Enlightenment
for Everyone

A PRACTICAL GUIDE

TO REALIZING

YOUR TRUE NATURE

Book Design
by Paul Ferrini and Lisa Carta

Cover Painting:
Buddha Under the Mango Tree
(circa 1025) Ch'ên Yung-Chih
Courtesy, Museum of Fine Arts, Boston © 2000
Reproduced with permission

Library of Congress Catalog Card Number: 00-106791
ISBN 1-879159-45-7

Manufactured in the United States of America

HEARTWAYS
PRESS
P.O. Box 99
Greenfield, MA 01302

Enlightenment
for
Everyone

Paul Ferrini

TABLE OF CONTENTS

LIST OF SPIRITUAL PRACTICES

introduction

by

Iyanla Vanzant

W hen you find a rare gem, you want to keep it close to you, protect it from harm, and share it only with a precious few who can appreciate the value of what you have found. Such is *not* the case when it comes to my discovery of the work of Paul Ferrini. It is my mission to make sure that as many people as possible are led to his spiritual gems.

Paul Ferrini is an important teacher in the new millennium. He us a gentle guide. He is a wise mystic. Reading his book *Love Without Conditions* was a major awakening for me. It called forth many things that I knew, but *knew not* how to say. Now, I order Paul's books by the caseloads. They are required reading for all of my students and the team of folks with whom I work.

Paul's writing both inspires us and challenges us to develop a deeper love for ourselves, for others and for God. His brilliance as a teacher lies in his ability to simplify the most difficult concepts so that we can understand them. In this book, Paul de-mystifies the concept of enlightenment, helping us to understand the light we each bring to our own spiritual journey. Enlightenment, as Paul describes it, is not some esoteric experience available only to yogis who meditate in mountain caves. It is an experience we all can have, because the *light* is already within us.

With the ever-changing roles we play and the demands of our lifestyles, few of us may feel enlightened. When we attempt to look within ourselves, grasping for a deeper sense of meaning and purpose, we find the darkness of our pain and the mystery of the Spirit.

That can be pretty frightening! It makes us shy away from too much self-inquiry. Instead, we try to see, find and follow the light of others. In so doing, we deny the existence of our own light. However, we soon learn that borrowed light doesn't last for long. Only our own light can lead us to the truth we long for in our lives.

It isn't easy to abide the darkness. I know; I have been there. But the light is there. It just takes a while till you see it. When you walk into a dark room, your eyes need time to adjust. But gradually, you begin to see what's there.

This book is a door opening to that room. Read it and do the spiritual practices that are presented here and you will begin to see and embrace the light within your heart. You will begin to bring it forward into the foreground of your consciousness. As you practice, day by day, hour by hour, you will begin to feel lighter and happier inside. The people around you will see this and feel this.

Once you are in touch with your own light, you become a beacon, a torch, a ray of sunshine for others. You become a witness to the power of love, self-acceptance and compassion. You know without a doubt that the light is in everyone and wherever you go, you see it and demonstrate it.

The beautiful little book you hold in your hands is a simple, profound spiritual instrument. It not only tells you the truth. It provides you with concrete practices that can help you realize that truth in your life. I know that you will find it as precious and as empowering as I have.

Iyanla Vanzant

part

1

*seeing
the light
within*

Enlightenment

Enlightenment is not something that we have to seek. Each one of us has the light within us. We just don't see it or trust it.

Enlightenment is not contingent on our finding the right teacher or having some kind of peak spiritual experience. Enlightenment is the realization of the light that is within us. It is the conscious recognition and acceptance of that light. Enlightenment is discovering who we already are and being it fully.

Nothing to Get

There's nothing that you need to get, find or acquire to be enlightened. You don't need a teacher or a guru. You don't need a priest or rabbi to intercede with God for you. You don't need a special technique or meditation practice. You don't need to memorize scripture or engage in esoteric breathing practices.

Looking for spirituality outside of yourself is a dead end. No teacher or preacher can give you the light. They can give you a breathing technique or a mantra or a special prayer, but they can't give you the light, because you already have it. When you realize that no one else out there is more spiritual than you are and you begin to turn your attention away from outer teachers, you take the lid off the pot and you begin to smell the stew. Suddenly, where there seemed only to be darkness, there is a flame burning.

That flame is your essence. It is the light within your heart. It is intimately connected to the flame within the heart of every single person on the planet. When you see and attend to the flame within your heart, you nurture your connection to all beings, and to God, the Great Being, which is manifest in all forms.

The Good News

So the good news is that there is nothing lacking in you. The same spark that is within the heart of Jesus, or Buddha, or Moses or Mohammed is in your heart too. The bad news is that there is nothing special about you. You don't have any exclusive claim to the light. Actually, that's good news too.

The truth is it's all good news. The light is within each one of us. Some of us do a good job of covering it over, but those who know how to look can see through our most ingenious disguises.

An enlightened person knows how to look. Having seen the light within self, s/he can see it within others.

When you see the light inside yourself, you become it. Then you look with the light and everything you see is full of light.

Enlightenment isn't Special

Enlightenment is the potential of all beings. All people have the light within. But some people do not believe that they have it or they do not believe that others have it. Not believing that they have the light or believing that they have it exclusively, they block their connection with the Source. The truth within is shrouded by the erroneous ideas that they accept.

Of course, as soon as false ideas are relinquished, truth can be seen. The light can been hidden or disguised, but it cannot be destroyed. It is ever-present and eternal. It simply awaits our willingness to recognize it as it is.

Removing the Blocks

So becoming enlightened is not a journey to find what we lack, but a journey to discover what we already have but do not recognize in ourselves and others. It is a journey of perception in which we learn to look through all the clever disguises we have adopted in an attempt to hide the truth from one another. It is a process of removing the blocks to our awareness of the spiritual flame—the presence of love—within our hearts and the hearts of others.

Becoming enlightened is a process of learning to live with an open heart and an open mind. And it is a process of surrendering all that closes our minds and our hearts: our judgments and fears, our prejudices, expectations, interpretations and defense mechanisms.

Letting Illusions Fall Away

If we are to become what we truly are, we must be willing to let go of what we are not. The false self must be surrendered for the true Self to be seen.

We aren't the person others think we are. We aren't the person our parents or spouses want us to be. We aren't the person society or church wants us to be.

We are not someone else's ideal. We are not even our own ideal.

All that is just froth that bubbles up when the wave crashes on the beach. It is the edge of the ocean, not its center. All images of self, whether they come from inside or outside, are powerless to describe the truth about you or me.

The Truth

The truth about us is beyond words and images. It can be experienced, but it cannot be easily described.

Once you have experienced the truth, names and forms mean very little. The name you give to truth or the form in which it appears means very little. One day truth has this name or form. The next day it has another.

Name and form cannot describe truth. At best they can point to it. At best, they are like the finger pointing to the moon.

The finger knows that it is not the moon. One who has experienced truth knows that he cannot describe it.

At best he can say "it is a little bit like that." But as soon as you try to capture it and imprison it in a name or form, he is forced to say "No, it is not like that, after all."

But rest easy. Truth is not something for which you must seek. It is not something that is separate from you. It is the essential aspect of who you are.

Just being yourself, truth is embodied. You don't have to try. You don't have to perform. You don't have to go to school. You are already it.

You were already it when you were born.

Leave your Nets

As a little one, you knew that you were the truth, but you knew nothing of the world. As soon as you started learning about the world, you started forgetting the truth about you.

By now, it is safe to say that, although you may be a proficient citizen of your world, you probably don't remember your spiritual identity. You have built a shell around your essence, and you don't know how to break through it. That shell is made of images of self and the beliefs and assumptions that arise from them. You are hypnotized by these images and live in their energy field as surely as the planets live in the gravitational pull of the sun and make their predictable orbit around it.

Any spiritual path worth its salt tells you that you must break through the shell if you want to see your original nature. It asks you to unlearn what you have learned about yourself and others. It asks you to undo what you have so carefully done.

Jesus tells you "Leave your nets." If you do not have the courage to cast your nets aside, you can spend the rest of your life preoccupied with what *is* or *is not* inside them. There is nothing wrong with this. It is simply the way of the world. You live on the surface. You never break through the self-created shell that keeps you apart from who you are.

The Inner Quest

The inner journey begins when you leave your nets or detach yourself from their contents. You withdraw from the world or you live in the world without being of the world.

Your focus ceases to be on what is happening outside of you. Instead, you become aware of the contents of your consciousness.

You notice how you are affected by external events. You notice how you are affected by your own internal mental and emotional states.

You stop investigating the world and begin to investigate

yourself. Your mind looks inward instead of outward. You sink down through layers of consciousness until you reach ground zero: the place where the original neurotic idea (*I am separate from the Source of Love*) was born, along with all of the self-betraying behaviors that accompany it.

Until this idea is challenged, your inner journey cannot begin. Thinking that you do not have the love you want, you look for love outside yourself. You try to find completion through others. But this search inevitably comes up empty, because no one else can give you the love that you already have. You just need to find your own love and trust it.

Often it takes a powerful external event such as the loss of a loved one to force you to turn inward to find the acceptance and completion you have always sought through others. You learn to take time to be with yourself, to listen to your guidance, to take risks, make mistakes, and to ask for help and forgiveness. You risk being yourself and stop giving your power away to others. This is the birthplace of spirituality. It is the manger where your infant self lies. It is your job to swaddle it, nurture it, watch it grow and come into its fullness. In this way alone is the master born.

There comes a time in each person's life when s/he can no longer pretend to be something s/he is not in the attempt to please parents, spouse, children or community. The second birth—the birth of the spiritual being—comes when we stop betraying our true Self and rise in the truth of who we are. This is the coming of the promised one. This is the savior.

S/he does not come from without. S/he does not come from on high. S/he does not come with lightning and thunder and beating of wings. S/he comes when the quiet voice is heard and trusted.

Such a gentle act turns lead into gold, and iron into steel. Inner gives birth to outer. The alchemical process of self-transformation begins.

As for the old self, it falls to pieces by itself. When the spirit is liberated, humpty dumpty comes off the wall and breaks into hundreds of meaningless pieces.

When the original false belief is corrected, all the assumptions and behaviors that belief supported come crashing down. Veritable skyscrapers implode in the mind. Whole cities return to pasture. The borders between countries dissolve.

The world made by self acceptance is a different world than the one made by self-hatred. It is a world of charity and peace. Not fighting ourselves, there is no fight to find in the world.

Mind as Luminary

It is the nature of mind to be full of light. An open mind lets the light in. It sees "what is."

Open mind is like a window pane. It lets the light come streaming through.

Closed mind—or fearful mind—blocks the light. It is literally a blind placed over the window. It is a mind that is made up, a mind with a prejudice or an agenda, a mind that judges what it sees.

Enlightenment means letting the light in, all of the light. It means open mind.

When your mind is open, you are full of light.

Like most people, you are enlightened in some moments and not in others. When fear arises, the window shade comes down. Don't be ashamed of this. Just be aware of it.

You are the one raising the shade and lowering it. Just be aware that you are the one who is doing it. Don't make anyone else responsible for what you see.

Be aware of the quality of your experience when mind is open and the quality of your experience when mind closes down. Don't beat yourself up when fear rises and your mind closes. Just notice what is happening without judging it.

The Doorkeeper

As you observe mind opening and closing, you witness the emotional states that accompany each phenomenon. Open mind keeps the heart open. Closed mind closes the heart.

Open mind brings trust, patience, resilience to the heart. When the mind is open, the heart is at peace.

Closed mind brings distrust, impatience, hyper-sensitivity to the heart. When the mind is closed, the heart is disturbed.

Open mind brings love and love in turn keeps the heart open.

Closed mind brings fear and fear in turn keeps the heart shut down.

Just remember, you are the doorkeeper.

If you cannot yet take responsibility for opening and closing the door, at least watch what happens to you when the door opens and closes.

Physical vs. Spiritual Light

Without physical light, we cannot see each other. We cannot differentiate one form from another. We cannot see each other's uniqueness.

Physical light helps us separate one form from another. It enables us to see accurately, to discriminate, to appreciate subtle differences. It also helps us individuate and appreciate our unique talents and creations.

Spiritual light is not at odds with physical light. It is not opposed to individuation. The acceptance of individual differences is essential for a spiritual perspective.

But spiritual light not only helps us see and accept differences. It also helps us recognize what we have in common. It helps us see how we are existentially equal to one another and how our lives are alike. When we see one another in spiritual light, we know that our experiences are different only on the surface. Beneath the surface, our stories are quite similar. Your joys and sorrows are the same as mine.

SEEING THE LIGHT WITHIN

When we look with the light, each form is luminous. One form may be a little different from another, but it is no more or less worthy. The light shows us the underlying worthiness and unity of all forms.

When seen in the light, there is no *me* that is more or less worthy than *you*. There is no *me* that is not connected to *you*. *I* can't be myself and not be connected to *you*. *I* can't be myself and not be as worthy as *you*.

Conditions

There are no conditions for enlightenment, except for the ones you bring.

If you think that you or anyone else is special, you won't be able to see the light within yourself or others. If you think that you are a victim of someone else's actions, if you blame yourself or if you blame others, if you hold onto guilt, judgments or resentments, you won't be able to see the light within yourself or others.

All the filters come from you.

You are the window blind or the window. It is your choice.

Just accept life as it unfolds and you are the clear window through which the light passes.

Simplicity

All this is so profoundly simple it goes totally past you. "I know that," you say, as if in anticipation that there is more coming. The problem is there is no more coming. This is it.

Open your heart and mind or don't open them. Those are your only choices. Each choice leads to a different experience.

Please experiment. Find out for yourself.

The search for more complicated truths may seem more compelling, but it leads back to the same place. Your choice remains the same: hide the light or let it shine through.

It's the same choice over and over again, moment by moment, breath by breath. Sorry folks. That's it.

That's why it all comes down to practice.

In this and every other chapter of this book there are spiritual exercises that you can practice on a daily basis. They will help you to verify experientially the simple concepts that are discussed in these pages.

PRACTICE 1
COMPASSIONATE SELF-ACCEPTANCE

We're all good at being the window shade. We've had plenty of training closing our hearts and our minds. So if we want to have a different experience, we have to be willing to try something new. How can we approach our experience in a new way?

First, let's find out if we can allow our experience to unfold without resisting it. Let's take five or ten minutes to be aware of our experience as it unfolds and see if we can accept what happens. If resistance comes up, let's be aware of the resistance without judging it. When judgments arise, let's hold them compassionately.

If you can accept your experience as it arises, that's wonderful. Feel the bliss of that acceptance. Feel the great expansiveness of being the window through which light passes.

If you judge or find fault with your experience, be aware of this and feel compassion for yourself. As you love yourself through your judgments, feel the expansiveness that happens in your heart. Instead of shutting up tight, as it usually does when judgments come up, feel your heart open up as you bring love and acceptance to yourself.

Practice this throughout the day. Do it two or three times per day for the first week. If you find it helpful, increase your practice periods. Do it two or three times per hour until it becomes a way of living. When you live in acceptance, your life is full of grace. When you live in compassion for yourself, your heart stays open, even when judgments arise.

PRACTICE 2
THE POWER OF NOT KNOWING

In our limited consciousness, we can't help thinking that we know what our experience means. However, the more we believe that we have the answers, the more our minds close to the mystery of our experience. Important insights and opportunities are missed because we are seeing our experience in a fixed or narrow way.

Today, practice not knowing what anything means. Just be with your experience without analyzing it or interpreting it. Be with the experience of others in the same way. Be neutral about your experience and that of others. Don't be for it or against it. Just accept it as it is and allow it to unfold.

If your judgments come up, be aware of them. Be aware of your tendency to beat yourself up for the judgments you have. Don't make it bad to have judgments. Don't make it good not to have judgments. Be with your experience without evaluating it.

Remember, today you are a professional **unknower**. You don't know what anything means: even ordinary things that you take for granted. Let everything be new. Let everything be free of your opinion, your judgment, your interpretation.

Practice this several times during the day. Practice it when you think you know what something means or when someone asks for your opinion. Ask yourself, "what is my experience like when it is free of the limitations I place upon it?"

If you find this practice helpful, use it on a regular basis. Let it become a way of being. Surrender what you know and live in the perpetual discovery of what remains.

part
2

*throwing
away
the mask*

Finding the River

If you did your practice exercises, you probably see now that life unfolds just beautifully when you drop your judgments and interpretations of it. Indeed, it unfolds just fine even when you are judging it if you don't get lost in your judgments. If you know that your judgments are just clouds passing by overhead or water moving under the bridge, then they have no power to upset you or detract from your experience. When you can refrain from deciding what something means, you can let it unfold and show you its meaning.

This takes patience. You can't be in a hurry. You can't be pressuring life to reveal itself. Life reveals itself when you allow it to, when you adjust your pace to coincide with its pace.

If you expect life to adjust to you, to meet your expectations, you will be pretty disappointed. The adjustments, for the most part, need to come from you. You are the one who needs to slow down and listen, the one who needs to let go of expectations, the one who needs to step back and get out of the way.

If you've made your mind up, if your expectations are fixed, if the position you've taken is a rigid one, you will be overruled. The River of Life will swiftly pass you by or unexpectedly sweep you away.

Life is in charge, not you or I. Life decides and you learn to abide with it, or you pay the price. Those who refuse to cooperate or adjust become the river's casualties.

The first question you need to answer on the spiritual path is "Who's in charge?" And the answer is "Not your ego, nor any one else's." The One who is in charge operates outside of your ego structure and that of others. Call it God, Self or River. The name does not matter.

You and every other person with an ego structure needs to surrender to that Divine Self, that River Within. If you don't, you will experience only struggle and hardship. That's because, no matter how strong your ego is, no matter how good you are at taking charge or making things happen, you are not as strong as the River is.

You will never win that fight. So better drop it from the get-go. Better surrender before you get bashed on the rocks. Or get bashed on the rocks, if you like. It's your choice.

Surrender

As long as you think it has to be your way, you haven't gotten it! You see, it cannot be your way. That's control. And you can't have control if you want to live a life of Spirit. Spirituality requires surrender. No, not to someone else. Not to your ego or anyone else's, but to the River that lies within you.

You see, you and everyone else out there is surrendering to the same River. You may give it different names or perceive it differently, but it is the same River.

The River's in charge. Your only choice is to fight its authority (an exhausting choice) or to surrender to it. Some people figure out right away that surrender is inevitable. For others, it takes years to figure out.

No matter. This is not a race to the finish line. There are no winners and losers in this game. But everybody has to play by the same rules.

And the first rule is: "You are not in charge." Of course, the "you" referred to here is the small "you" of your ego structure, not the big "You" that has merged with the River. It's the you that's just learning how to swim, not the amphibious you that is as comfortable on water as on dry land.

The Emotional Body

You've probably heard people say they try to "go with the flow." Unfortunately, they do so while standing on the riverbank. There is no way you can know what it means "to go with the flow" until you jump into the river. Of course, the moment your body hits the water and feels the current, this law becomes totally obvious. Once you are in the water, you can't do anything except in relationship to the current.

The water we're talking about here is the "emotional body." It is the place where feelings are activated. Until you learn to understand and navigate through your emotional body, spiritual growth is a rather abstract, intellectual proposition. You can read all the right books and say all the right things, but still feel suicidal or rage out in front of your partner or your children. The current you experience in the emotional body is your desire energy: the pull and push of what you want and don't want, along with your past hurts, wounds, resentments and grievances. It is a turgid, rumbling, watery mass of contradictory feelings. No one can predict what it will do when its waters are stirred up.

So when we say "go with the flow" we aren't kidding. You don't have any choice. Whatever you feel must be experienced. And it's always better to experience the feeling right now than it is to stuff the feeling. Feelings that are dammed up erupt with greater ferocity when the emotional blockage is removed.

To feel your feelings you need to slow down and tune in on a regular basis. This is not something that most people know how to do. Usually, when you feel an emotion, you try to get rid of it. If you feel anger, you try to give it to someone else. If you feel sadness, you try to overcome it. If you are willing to feel the anger or the sadness, you can get in touch with what lies behind them.

To feel the feeling, you have to jump into the river. You have to act like a fish. You can't stand on the bank with a fishing pole.

Taking time to accept and explore your anger, hurt, sadness, peace, and your joy helps you connect more deeply with life. You anchor in your experience, instead of running off to the next thing. As a result, you are able to use that experience as fuel for your growth toward individuation and building healthy relationships with others.

PRACTICE 3
FEELING YOUR FEELINGS

Today, you are going to feel your feelings. If you are at work and something comes up that upsets you, you are not going to push it under the carpet. You are going to take some time to get in touch with how you are feeling. You do this not to try to "fix" anything or to try to make the feeling go away. You do it to experience the feeling fully!

That means focusing not so much on what triggers you as on how you are being triggered. It means allowing the wave of emotion to wash through you and bring up whatever material is ready to be made conscious.

Today, you are not going to stuff your feelings and go on to the next thing. Today, you are going to take the time to experience how you feel. If you feel anger, recognize it and say "I can feel this anger. Is there anything else behind it?" And if sadness lies behind the anger, ask "Is there anything behind this sadness?" Keep asking and exploring until you come to the bottom of the emotion you are feeling. When you get to the bottom, stay there. Feel what you need to feel until you feel the emotion shift. When you give your feelings the attention they deserve, they naturally move toward integration and wholeness.

Today, no matter how many feelings come up for you, you

are going to take the time to feel them all. Today, you are going to spend the whole day in the river. And you are going to begin to tune into the current and see how it influences everything you think and do in your life.

Denial isn't a River

There are two extreme ways of dealing with your feelings. One is to try to hide them, or to stuff them. The other is to wallow in them and let them take over your life. Both are methods of denial.

The first method is dishonest to yourself and others, but it can work for some time. Your pretense can fool even your closest friends. But then something unexpected happens and the tidal wave erupts. The lie becomes visible. People are shocked. The person they knew isn't standing before them anymore.

Denial wastes a lot of time: your time and other people's time. It's better to be honest with yourself and others about how you feel, even though this may be an uncomfortable thing to do. If other people walk away when you tell the truth, so be it. In the end, they would have found out the truth, even if you had twisted yourself into a pretzel trying to please them. Trying to please others is one of the classic ways of running away from your own feelings.

Projection is another form of denial. If you don't want to feel an emotion like anger, you project it onto someone else. You draw an angry person into your life. Then, you can self-righteously attack that person while totally forgetting that it's your own anger you are attempting to push away. Instead of accepting your anger, you reject it and try to give it to someone else.

Some people try to hide or disguise their feelings. Others stay stuck in their feelings for days. This may manifest as chronic depression or anxiety, or as a kind of obsessive clinging to the past. You allow the feeling to overwhelm you and you give your power to it. Actually this too is a subtle, albeit paradoxical, form of denial, because you don't attend to the feeling, but lose yourself in it.

Whether your form of denial of feelings is to stuff them, project them onto someone else, or become engulfed in them, you are not attending to your feelings. Don't feel embarrassed by these tendencies to push your feelings away. They are learned behavior and are constantly reinforced by the culture in which we live. Instead, be aware that you are pushing your feelings away. The more awareness you bring to the ways in which you avoid feelings, the easier it will be for you to face your feelings as they arise.

Whenever you find yourself withdrawing emotionally from others, you can be sure that you have feelings coming up that you don't want to deal with. The same is true when you are angry at or critical toward others. Whatever you need to hide or give to someone else belongs to you and needs to be looked at.

You can be sure that acknowledging your feelings is a revolutionary act. When you take notice of how you feel and own it to yourself and others, you destroy the land-mines you or someone else might step on in the future.

Everybody has feelings s/he is ashamed of. You are not alone in this. You are not being asked to give your power away to these negative emotions. Rather, you are being asked to bring these feelings into your conscious awareness so that they don't explode when you least expect it.

Attending to the emotional body is necessary spiritual work. It takes practice.

So please practice. Be aware when you deny how you feel and take time to feel your feelings. Give yourself plenty of slack. This isn't an easy thing to do.

Uniting Head and Heart

There is a kind of knowing that comes from resting in the river. It is a very different kind of knowing than the kind that comes from standing on the shore. Both types of knowing are important.

When you stand on the shore, you can see the sweep of the river in both directions. You see storms brewing at the horizon's edge and boats approaching from the channel. You appreciate the whole field of possibilities. You can see the big picture.

When you rest in the river, you feel the current. You know what you are experiencing right now. You know what feels right and what doesn't. You feel relaxed and safe or you feel vulnerable and scared. You understand the reality immediately at hand.

You can't live life successfully without both types of knowing. You need to see the big picture with its panorama of possibilities and you need to be aware of how you feel right now.

If you try to act without checking in with your emotional body, you will push the envelope in vain. You may rush off into outer space without realizing there is a giant rubber band on your foot. That rubber band never lets you do something you don't feel comfortable doing. It always brings you back to reality.

If you act without checking in, you may blast off in a great cloud of glory, but you soon fall flat on your face. The rubber band always wins. The river always triumphs.

By all means see the big picture. Use it to guide you as you respond to the specific requirements of the moment. But keep checking within. If something doesn't feel right, pay attention. Then you have the best of both worlds.

The idea is not to merge with your emotions and let them run you, but to link thought and emotion so that mind and heart work together. Try on new ideas and see how they feel. Observe emotions as they arise and play themselves out.

Don't cut off your right arm because it is stronger than your left or your left because it is stronger than your right. Develop the non-dominant side. Work toward balance and equality. That's how you integrate masculine and feminine, reason and intuition, head and heart.

See the big picture and the small picture. Dive into the river and swim. Then get out and let your eyes gaze along the riverbank.

Let your heart be open enough to take in all of your ideas. Let your mind be open enough to consider all of your feelings. Know in your heart as well as in your head. Allow your consciousness to be the creative synthesis of thought and feeling, reason and emotion. Let it be the furnace in which the alchemical metals fuse together.

Be the alchemist at work. Learn from your mistakes. Turn the lead of your experience into spiritual gold.

Do not be impulsive or impatient with the process. Allow time for the sky to drink from the river. Be patient while the clouds gather and come down to sit on the mountains. Be the thirsty cornfields waiting for rain. You are the ground of being in which the miracle of life is unfolding.

Authenticity

Authenticity comes from telling the truth about how you think and feel. If you keep your thoughts secret and don't take time to feel your feelings, you can't be honest with yourself or others.

You will wear a mask in your interactions with others and that mask will disguise your experience, instead of revealing it. Intimacy cannot happen when the truth of your experience cannot be shared.

You might proudly display your persona, participating in the social life your community, without revealing who you are to anyone. This is a life of pretense, a life that is a lie to yourself and others.

Being authentic can be messy and even unsavory at times. Our thoughts and feelings aren't always pleasant. But disguising how we think and feel doesn't let others know where we are coming from. They make assumptions about us that aren't true. They have an unrealistic idea of who we are and what they can expect from us. And we are forced to live with the guilt of misleading others and the fear of letting the cat out of the bag.

Sooner or later, the mask rips and our real thoughts and feelings reveal themselves. This can be shaming to us and unnerving, if not hurtful, to others.

No matter how elaborately it is disguised, the truth always reveals itself in the end. Why not tell the truth now, and face our fears head on, instead of burying the truth and living in perpetual fear of every little tremor we feel underfoot.

It takes courage to be authentic. It takes courage to spill the beans when we know the other person hates beans. But if beans are all you have, why pretend that they are grapes?

People aren't as stupid as we sometimes think they are. They know when things don't add up and their intuition helps them see beyond our words into our hearts.

The nature of secrets is that they are revealed. Lies can cover up the truth for a while, but in the end those lies wear thin.

When push comes to shove, we have no choice. We have to

be who we are. We get worn out trying to be somebody else.

Why waste a lot of time and energy in lies and deceptions? Why pretend to be something other than yourself?

In the end, you return home. You come into this life naked and you go out naked. It doesn't matter how many costumes you have worn in between.

An enlightened person is content to be who s/he is. S/he doesn't need to please anybody else. S/he doesn't need disguises.

An enlightened person tells the truth, because the truth is simple and stands by itself. Lies are complicated and need constant uplifting and support.

An enlightened person lives a simple life without lies or disguises. What you see is what you get.

Such people are easily passed over in our rush to fall at the feet of "the beautiful people" who have the best disguises and the most toys. But enlightened people don't mind. They aren't looking for an audience or a following.

They know better than that.

PRACTICE 4
TELLING THE TRUTH

Today, make an effort to be in touch with your experience and share it honestly with others. Don't deny your feelings or lie to others about what you are thinking and feeling. On the other hand, don't use the truth to beat up on others or on yourself. Tell the truth gently and with compassion. Use it as a bridge that you cross in the dance of intimacy. Invite people to meet you half way. Reveal something about yourself and perhaps others will trust you with their own truth.

Today, be willing to take off your mask. Be willing to look into people's eyes and people's hearts, if they invite you in. Be willing to invite others in if they approach you with love and respect.

No, don't be an exhibitionist ripping off your clothes as you walk down the street. Don't shout your truth from the rooftops or yell it into people's ears on the subway. Compulsive confessing is not self-disclosure. It is another type of mask.

Today, see the mask for what it is: a way of protecting yourself from hurt, ridicule and unwanted attention. Do not expose yourself if it doesn't feel safe. Wear the mask when you need it. But look for times when it is safe to take the mask off. Take baby steps into revealing yourself, into letting others know who you are. Intimacy is not possible without authentic self-disclosure.

When you find that you are holding back information that other people need to have, find a way to start talking about it, even if it seems a bit awkward. When someone confides in you, return the favor. When people tell you the truth even though they admit that they are embarrassed or scared, they are opening the door for you. Don't miss the opportunity to walk through the open door.

It isn't easy to open the door when it has been closed for a long time. If it opens by itself, scoot through it. Open your mouth and say what needs to be said. Trust the words that come to you at the time. They don't have to be perfect.

When you act with courage, it is not the words that are important, but the intent behind the words. People feel that. They know that you are doing the best that you can.

Today's exercise is not an invitation to blurt out inappropriate or hurtful things to others. It is an invitation to speak that which has been too long withheld, that which is heavy on your heart, the truth that has been felt but not told. Today is not about hasty speaking, but about speaking the unspoken words you have heard over and over again in your head. Today is not about shocking others or speaking in an offensive way. It is a gentle offering from your heart to another's. Today is about sharing. It is about trust. It is about voicing an anger or a hurt or asking a forgiveness. It is about softening and meeting your partner half way. It is about walking with open heart and arms extended to the center of the bridge. It is about meeting others in the fullness of your own truth.

part
3

*living
in the
present*

The Present Moment

The present is a timeless space. It has no sequence, no goal, no process. It merely is what it is.

Live in the present and what need do you have for beliefs or theories? What concern do you have about yesterday or tomorrow?

Living in the present is effortless, that is to say it takes no more effort than you spontaneously give to it. You don't have to labor to be present. Nobody can come to you and tell you "You need to work harder at living in the present."

It is easy to live in the present because all it demands of you is your awareness and your attention. As soon as you lose your awareness or attention, you move out of the present.

As a simple practice, try living in the present for five minutes. Don't concern yourself with what happened yesterday, an hour ago, or even five minutes ago. Just be present now. If you find yourself thinking about the past, just be aware of it. If you find yourself thinking about the future, just be aware of it.

Being present for five minutes does not seem like such a difficult task, but it is profoundly difficult for most people. Most people are constantly looking back at the past or forward to the future. Their thoughts and emotions are not focused on this moment, but on some other one. As a result, there is very little present awareness or ability to meet life as it unfolds.

One of the best ways to stay present in this moment is to take a deep breath, release it and then spend several minutes breathing consciously. Why don't you try this for the next five minutes? As soon as you find your mind wandering, bring your awareness back to your breathing.

When you are focused on something that is happening in the present—i.e. your breath—your consciousness stays present, instead of floating off to the remembered past or the anticipated future. Breathing is a great way to connect with what's happening right now, but it's not the only way.

Another way to connect with the present is to witness the thoughts that are going through your mind. Imagine that your thoughts are moving forward like a self propelled wheelbarrow and you are walking behind them seeing where they are going. You aren't trying to direct them. The wheelbarrow is moving by itself. You are just intensely curious to see where the wheelbarrow is going.

This may seem like an awkward analogy, but being a witness or observer is sometimes an awkward role for us. We are used to taking charge or letting someone else take charge. We are used to pushing the wheelbarrow or getting in it and letting someone else push it. But walking behind a self-propelled wheelbarrow seems a bit strange.

The whole point is that being the witness requires that your consciousness neither direct your thoughts nor be directed by them. If you identify with your thoughts, you will be taken on a whirlwind ride. You will be inside the wheelbarrow, a participant rather than an observer. By contrast, if you try to take control and think only certain thoughts, you will be pushing the wheelbarrow. You will be invested in the outcome of your own actions, instead of just curious about what's happening.

To be curious about what's happening is to be alert or aware. You are neither for nor against. You are just present for what's happening. That's the state of consciousness meditation takes us to: aware but not attached.

Any time you start paying attention to what is happening in the present moment, you can move into ecstatic awareness. For example, if someone is talking and you listen deeply without having an opinion or taking sides, you make direct heart contact with the person who is speaking. You don't have to say a word and the person feels heard.

We tend to make spirituality a heady, intellectual proposition, but it really isn't. It's just becoming present: breathing, being in our bodies, listening to others when they speak, putting one foot in front of another on the trail. There's nothing complicated about it. You can have just as much awareness cleaning latrines as you can discussing the *General Theory of Relativity*. Maybe more.

Spiritual awareness is not glamorous or esoteric. It is everyday stuff.

As long as we think otherwise, we spend a great deal of time up in our heads trying to figure things out and solve everybody's problem. It is futile, exhausting work. Then one day, out of sheer frustration, we just give it all up and get a job driving a trolley car. The tumble down into our hearts is a journey of intense and peculiar genius, like the experience of Samuel Beckett's Malloy throwing away all his sucking stones after he has tediously and painstakingly moved them from pocket to pocket, sucking each one in the right order.

Some of us approach our spirituality in the same way until, one day, like Malloy, we just go crazy and start pulling those stones out of our pockets and heaving them in any direction on the beach. When we leave thinking behind, heavenly choirs rejoice. The funny thing is we never knew they existed until we started cleaning the latrines!

PRACTICE 5
FOLLOWING THE WHEELBARROW

Today, keep your consciousness in your belly, your heart, or your toes. If you have wood, chop it. If you have a garden, dig in it. Do what is before you with your full attention. If your mind wanders, take a deep breath and bring your attention back to this moment.

Don't get lost in your thoughts or try to direct them. Just be aware of whatever thoughts or feelings arise and see where they go. Be a witness to whatever is happening. Be curious, but don't analyze or take sides. Just be present, physically, emotionally, intellectually. When you are present on all these levels, you are spiritually engaged.

Today, be present as a tree is present in the forest or as a fish is present in the sea. Go about your business with clarity and focus. Don't dream and scheme. Don't plan. Just stay where you are and do what you can do. As you walk, be aware of the breeze against your cheek. Notice the sun when it goes behind the clouds and when it reappears, sending a shaft of light down to earth.

Today, just be aware and alert to whatever you experience. Don't go up into your head. Stay in your heart. Breathe and be in your body. Stretch and breathe. Forget about tomorrow or yesterday. Be here right now.

Psychological time

You live in psychological time when your focus leaves the present and goes into the past or future. Psychological time happens in your own mind. You can be thinking about the breakup of your last relationship while you are eating dinner with friends, or you can be wondering what will happen when you go on vacation next week while you are lifting weights at the gym. In both cases, you are physically present without being present mentally or emotionally. To some degree, you have dissociated from the present moment.

Dissociation takes you from existential time into psychological time. In psychological time all kinds of things can be happening for you that aren't happening for anyone else. Psychological time is not social. It is solitary and solipsistic.

53

Psychological time is not rhythmic like existential time. The sun does not rise and set, the moon does not go through her phases, and the seasons do not occur in psychological time.

Psychological time is inhabited only by you. Trees and rocks and streams do not live there, nor do other people. It is not relational. Psychological time is created and destroyed in your consciousness alone. It can't be shared.

Most if not all of the suffering you experience happens in psychological time. In other words, it happens only when your consciousness leaves the present moment.

Timelessness

You can't suffer if you meet the present fully. In the present there is only bliss.

Time passes in the present, but it is not the kind of time that you measure with your watch. It is the kind of time that is measured by the passing of the clouds overhead or the disappearing of the sun in the western sky at dusk. It is rhythmic time, the time of the beating of the river on the rock or the stick on the drum.

This time is timeless. It comes and it goes eternally.

When you abide in the present, you live in the timeless dimension of experience. You live in the place where the river within and the river without meet. You are the crossroads.

This is where the Sabbath is celebrated: in the present

moment. It cannot be celebrated when consciousness dwells in the past or future.

PRACTICE 6: SABBATH RITUAL

Today, retreat from psychological time. Do not pick up the phone to make a call. Do not get in your car to go to the store. Instead, be quiet and breathe. Be quiet and listen. Walk by a river or a stream. Be in the flow of your life. Be the crossroads, where life within meets life without.

Do not plan what you will do. Just do what occurs to you as it occurs. Do it with poise and simple dignity. Do not rush. Do not labor. Just allow your day to unfold as it naturally does.

Accept what comes to you. Don't resist your experience. Be in the river and trust it. Let it take you where it needs to go.

Do this for a day and see how you feel. Do it for several days, for a week or a month. Retreat from psychological time and enter the fullness of this moment.

Sacred time is underneath your eyelids and right beneath your feet. The Sabbath is celebrated with the next breath. You don't need to find a formal time or place to worship. Here and now will do just fine.

part

4

*gratitude
and
praise*

Let the Gift Reveal Itself

To be grateful, you must first accept what happens. Even if it seems to be difficult, you must find a way to get your arms around it. Tell yourself "God does not give questionable gifts." If something is in your life, it has a purpose. You might not know what that purpose is, but that's okay. Accept what comes to you and its purpose will reveal itself to you.

Acceptance leads naturally to the unfolding of purpose. Don't be impatient. Don't judge the contents of your life too harshly. Don't make up your mind about what something means prematurely. Just let it be and learn to be with it.

God does not bring punishment into your life. S/He brings only gifts. They may not seem like gifts to begin with, but if you live with them for a while, you'll learn the lesson that they bring. Lessons learned are gifts received.

"Thanks for the lesson, God," you'll learn to say. "I don't know how else I would have gotten it."

So remember, what looks like a kick in the derriere might really be a gift, if you can come to terms with it. Don't be so quick to reject your experience. Accept it. Live with it. And let it reveal itself to you.

Giving Thanks

When you celebrate life, you get the most joy out of it. So celebrate what happens. Tell your friends "I don't know why I'm so happy—God knows, my life is a total mess—but I just can't help it."

Dance while the city is burning. And then dance on the ashes. Without the fire, we couldn't rebuild. Endings are sad, but they lead to beginnings. "Dear God, thanks for the ending. It gave me a new beginning. I will always be grateful."

Your life is a prayer that is spoken for God. And there is never a moment when God is not listening. So pray without ceasing, even if it means you have to say "Why me, God?" or "Why did you give me lemons when you know I hate lemonade?"

Keep talking to God. Keep remembering that God loves you even though S/He sometimes chooses strange ways to show you that love.

Keep dancing, even if you don't like the tune. It's only a matter of time before a tango turns into a polka, or a waltz into a gigue.

To be grateful, you must know that you are loved and appreciated no matter what happens. You must be deeply convinced of your own goodness. You must know without a doubt that you are worthy. Then, you receive everything that happens as a blessing. And when you bless what comes to you, it becomes incapable of harming you in any way.

This is what it means to be a man or a woman of peace. Peace is in your heart and all that happens gets brought into that heart and it becomes peaceful.

It's all Good

After God created heaven and earth, he looked around and saw that "it is good." He didn't say "It's all good except for the worms and the buzzards." He didn't say "I like everybody but that fellow Satan." He said "It's all good."

So if that's how God feels about His Creation, who are we to complain about what happens in our lives? Maybe it's time to learn from the master builder that "It's all good," even the worms, the buzzards, and the devils.

Like God, we create all kinds of things, but we don't like our creations as well as God likes His. We make things that hurt us or reduce the quality of our lives. And then we feel bad, sad, or mad about it. We haven't gotten very skilled at recycling old creations and making new things we enjoy.

But with a little loving, our creations get more loveable. It's a process. The more we love what we do, the more we learn to enjoy what we create. Then we get to look at things the way God does and say "It's all good."

Now there's a little trick to this. Start saying "It's all good," and you will begin to believe it. And then anything you do seems just fine. You stop beating yourself up. You stop worrying about what other people think about you.

Saying "It's all good" is a self fulfilling prophecy. Say it and it comes into being.

PRACTICE 7
GRATITUDE FOR WHAT IS

Today, understand that whatever comes into your life is "good" and give thanks for all the good things in your life. Today, be grateful for life as it is, even though it does not meet your expectations, even though it doesn't fit into your ego-structure.

Today, don't just accept life as it comes. Be grateful for it. Find something to celebrate and praise in every word, every gesture, every situation.

Today, be positive, encouraging, upbeat, enthusiastic. No matter how seemingly negative a situation seems, be optimistic. See the best in it.

Don't just pretend to be positive. Let yourself feel it. Put some emotion into your praise and celebration. And don't keep your feelings inside.

Tell people how you feel. Tell people about the beauty and magnificence you see.

Today, be the representative of a loving and caring God.

Appreciate people. Tell them how much they mean to you. Tell them you like how they dress or the way they throw a baseball. Praise their smile or their patience.

Be grateful for each thing that happens today. Imagine that it is sent to you directly by God for your blessing. And give your blessing freely, even if you have no idea how such a thing could be positive.

Today, find a place to stash your negativity. Put on your cheerful clothes and think some upbeat, helpful thoughts. And don't forget your smile when you go out the door.

Today is God's day and you are the messenger of its abundance. Today, you are bringing people to the harvest. Today, you are inviting everyone to celebrate and give thanks.

And if you like doing it, you can do the same thing tomorrow, and the next day, and the next, and the next....

part
5

*seeing
the light
within
others*

Something Wrong?

If the light is already in us and there is nothing that we must do to become enlightened, then why are we here? Some people say that we are here to undo everything that we did in ignorance; we have made a mess and we have a lot of work to do to clean it up. They think that it's time to get busy.

But wait a minute. If we get busy trying to fix something that we think we did wrong, isn't it possible that we will make a worse mess than the one we already have? When have we ever made anything better than it is?

Maybe it's time to question our perception that something is wrong and needs to be fixed.

Another Theory

There is another way to view life than as a mess that needs to be cleaned up or a problem that needs to be solved. It's a radical theory and most people just laugh at it. That's too bad, because they dismiss a way of viewing life that could lead to genuine happiness.

This radical theory stipulates that "things are okay the way they are." It includes the corollaries: "You are okay the way you are and I am okay the way I am." It assumes that nobody needs to be fixed and recognizes that seeing problems and trying to fix them does not lead to happiness.

Challenges

The theory finds its greatest challenge in questions like "If things are great the way they are, what do we do when Hitler crosses into Czechoslovakia?"

Hitler and anyone else who thinks that there is a problem that needs to be fixed obviously doesn't accept the theory proposed here. So this question will continue to arise as long as one human being continues to take advantage of another one.

Moreover, questions like this seem to answer themselves and lead to beliefs like "some people are evil," which in turn provide the justification—fabricated although it may be—for destroying certain people in the name country, culture, religion or "love."

Many years ago Moses was given ten commandments and told that the Jews could live in peace and harmony if they would only abide by these commandments. They were simple ideas designed to keep the peace like "not stealing, lying, killing or sleeping with your neighbor's husband or wife." But it turned out that these commandments were not so easy for people to keep.

A couple of thousand years later, Jesus saw what a hard time people were having keeping these commandments. So he said, "Okay, ten are obviously too many for you guys to remember, so here's just two: "love God and love one another." Of course he had to add "even your enemies." Apparently, that "love your enemies part" was a bit much to ask.

So not much has changed when it comes to the interpersonal

relations front. People are still lying, stealing, raping and killing. And every single one of them has some justification for his actions. "It was the other guy's fault; he hit me first," they all say. A few even claim that "God" told them to do it, if you can believe that!

So here we are. We still think the reason we don't get along is because of what someone else does to us. We don't want to take responsibility for our own actions. We don't want any commandments to keep.

How You See Others

So what do you do when your brother assaults you? Do you defend yourself? And, if so, can you do so without dehumanizing him, without making him evil and casting him out of your heart?

The question is: what do you see in him? Do you see the light or the window shade? It doesn't matter that he is holding the shade down. Most people who harm others wear a mask over their faces. They don't want to be seen. They don't want to be recognized or loved, because they can't hurt you if they feel your love.

What do you see in your brother or sister, innocence or guilt, goodness or evil? If you believe in evil, you will close down your heart. You will do what Hitler did. You will put a mask over your head and push the genocidal trigger.

And don't think Hitler is just some crazed lunatic who lived in the past. Every generation has its Hitlers and the henchmen and women who carry out their fearful agendas.

Turning the Other Cheek

Now imagine for a moment that your brother is okay the way he is. But he doesn't believe it, so he attacks you. You have a choice, you can reinforce his guilt or remind him of his innocence.

If you remind him that he is okay the way he is, you reinforce your belief in yourself and in him, indeed in the innate goodness of all people. This is what it means to turn the other cheek.

Some people can't help acting out their inner sense of unworthiness. They project their inadequacy and attack others. They wear a sign saying "I am a bad person." And most people respond "Yes, you are."

But does Jesus or Gautama respond like this? No, because they see with the light and all they see is light. They don't see "bad person." They don't see "unworthy." They see one who suffers because he does not see the light within himself. And they say "Look, friend, this light that is in me is also in you."

When you establish in the truth, untruth will constantly present itself to you. Hitler will arise again and again and look you in the face. And if it isn't Hitler, it will be the one who is trying to kill Hitler.

As soon as one person is seen as evil, illusion reigns within the mind of the perceiver. And it promotes itself to all who would listen to its fearful voice.

This world is not divided by the struggle between good and evil—because evil does not exist—but by the struggle between the belief in evil and the belief in goodness. What is your belief?

PRACTICE 8
LOOKING FOR HITLER

Today be aware of your response to each person who comes into your life. Are you judging that person or accepting him or her? Don't try to change anything in your experience. Just be aware of it.

Maintain your awareness even when you are reading a newspaper or watching the news on TV. What is your response to the dictator who is killing innocent people? Do you find him innocent or guilty?

What is your response to your daughter when she interrupts your quiet time or to your spouse when s/he complains about something you did? Just be aware of how you respond to the people in your life. Do you bless them or curse them? Do you appreciate them or put them down?

See how you respond. See what you offer.

Who are the Hitlers in your experience? Do you dismiss anyone as evil? Is there someone in your life whom you perceive as unworthy of your acceptance and your love? If so, take a closer look at what you object to in that person. It may be that you see qualities in this person which you see and dislike in yourself.

This practice will help you identify those situations in which you find it difficult to give or receive love. Gradually you will learn to detect your fear as it arises, so that you can bring love and acceptance to yourself. Then, you won't so easily be triggered by what others say or do.

When you are at peace, you don't lose your peace even when you meet Hitler on the street. When there are no buttons to push, your blessing goes out unconditionally to everyone. You do not withhold your love from those who need it most, even when they are getting your attention in the most obnoxious or offensive ways.

Peace is an inside job. When your peace comes from within, nothing external can threaten it. When your peace comes from without, when it depends on how others treat you, almost any-one can take it away from you, even if they did not intend to.

Facing your Fears

When you see problems and think that you have to fix them, you live your whole life in reaction to what happens around you. You are driven from one extreme to the other. You live in perpet-ual stress and conflict.

By contrast, when you accept life the way it is and take responsibility for what you think and feel, you are centered and peaceful. When you are triggered by someone or something outside you, you immediately take responsibility for your reactivity. You don't try to make it anyone else's fault that you momentarily went into fear and lost your peace.

Living in awareness doesn't mean that fear ceases to come up for you. That's too much to expect from any enlightened person, including yourself. Fear continues to come up, but you deal with it differently. You don't try to push it off onto others. You meet it head-on with compassion and confidence. You know that when you hold your fear in compassionate awareness it has no power over you or anyone else.

By taking responsibility for your fear, you stop projecting it. You don't need to see evil personified outside of you. You begin to integrate your unconscious, shadowy material. As you feel whole within, old wounds start to heal.

You recognize the fear of others for what it is. You know others attack you only because they cannot love themselves. And you don't want to act in a way that makes them more fearful. So, whatever you do, you send them love.

Your little child who knows the fear, the hurt and the pain, sends love to the little child in others. Compassion is extended. You can face the pain of others, because you have faced your own pain time and time again.

The time for seeing and reacting to enemies is over. Now you see only brothers and sisters in pain who are calling out for your love and acceptance. And that is what you learn to give.

When you see no evil, you put an end to struggle and strife. You have only good things to say to and about others. You see only the light, even when it is shrouded in darkness. And light is what you reinforce, because light itself is the answer. No other answer can heal your wounds. Seen in light, no wound can remain unhealed, for the part cannot remain separate from the whole when the whole comes to embrace it.

PRACTICE 9
SEEING WITH LIGHT

Today, practice seeing everything in the light. When you see the part, remember the whole. When darkness presents itself, remember the light that lies behind it.

When someone is trying to fix a problem, don't interrupt him and tell him he's going about it all wrong. Don't try to fix the fixers. Don't remind them there's nothing to fix. Remind yourself.

Today, remember the light that lives in your heart and see others with this light. See the original nature in others, not the mask they wear to protect themselves.

Today, see the hand of God in everything and you will become the extension of that hand.

How can you be enlightened if you are unwilling to be the light? Be the light today.

If you can't do it now, you'll never be able to do it. So don't wait. Do it today. See only light today and be the light. Be God's loving hand and blessing upon all things that come into your life.

Guilty or Innocent

Remember, it all comes down to the question, "Do you see this person as guilty or innocent, evil or good." And we are not talking only about terrorists on the news. We are talking about your spouse, your child, or your parent.

Whenever you see an enemy, you create strife. You are no longer seeing with the light. You have been fooled by the mask the other person is wearing. You have been taken in, hoodwinked! You don't see the other person as s/he really is.

You approached the darkness, but forgot to bring the light. Since the other person has forgotten who s/he is, is it any wonder that darkness prevails?

Someone has to wake up and remember if sanity is to return. Remember who you are, and you will also remember who the other person is. Remember who the other person is, and you will remember who you are. Whether you see in darkness or in light, you always see the other person as you see yourself.

Self-crucifixion

Jesus was crucified by people who did not know who he really was. They saw the mask, not the real person. We crucify one another for the same reason.

What we don't realize initially is that all attack against others is an attack against ourselves. In our anger, we think we are striking out at others, but it is ourselves we hurt the most. Every negative thought we have and every negative action we take toward another causes continued suffering for us.

Each one of us must live with the fruits of our actions. We reap the rewards of our labors. Every action we take has a consequence for us.

That is why the Hindu religion advocates Ahimsa or "harmlessness." Using this simple idea, Ghandi led the Indian people to overthrow British colonial rule and Martin Luther King led a powerful movement promoting racial equality in the United States.

To practice Ahimsa means to live in a way that does not hurt others. It is to know in the core of our being that taking advantage of others cannot in any way improve the quality of our lives. Indeed, it can lead only to resentment, remorse and guilt.

PRACTICE 10
HARMLESSNESS

Today, practice Ahimsa (harmlessness) and the Golden Rule: "Do unto others as you would have them do unto you."

Whenever you are about to attack another person for any reason, remember that you are about to crucify yourself. It is impossible to hurt someone else without hurting yourself. Tune into this before you speak or act.

Refrain from speech and actions that are hurtful and then ask yourself, "How would I like to be treated if I were this person?" First, do no harm. Then, say the words and take actions you would like to receive if you were in the other person's position.

Practice this throughout the day and see what results you get. Not only will others be much happier with you, but you will be much happier with yourself. Make it an ongoing part of your spiritual practice and you will constantly find the light in yourself and in others.

If not Now, When?

Rabbi Hillel asked "If I am not for myself, who is for me? But if I am for myself alone, who am I?"

You cannot be happy if you do not see the light within yourself, nor can you be happy if you don't see the light within others. These two go together.

See the light in others and it is easier to feel good about yourself. See the light in yourself, and it is easier to feel compassion for others.

You have heard the expression "charity begins at home." You can't love the people of the world until you can love yourself, your family and your friends. Love extends outward in ever widening circles. It begins with your ability to hold yourself gently and compassionately. If you cannot do that, then this is where your spiritual work begins.

Of course, there will always be people who stand a little bit beyond your willingness to love and accept. But gradually, your arms will open even to them. Your embrace will continue to expand. And as it expands outward, it also expands inward.

Rabbi Hillel asked "If not now, when?" If we don't love ourselves or the people in front of us right now in this moment, when are we going to love them?

Love doesn't happen in the future. It happens right now. Right now, there is some part of yourself you are judging that wants to be accepted and loved. Right now there is someone you have rejected or pushed away who wants to come into your arms.

Love, not Agreement

It is easy to love people who agree with us and support us. However, it isn't so easy to love the people who are critical of us and say negative things to others about us.

Jesus, who gave us the "heart path" to enlightenment, encouraged us to love our enemies. Surely, he knew how difficult a proposition that was. Yet he required it of us anyway.

Why? Because we cannot ever come to peace so long as there is hatred in our hearts. We cannot be the light and harbor judgments and grievances. We must confess our negative thought and feeling states. We must release them if we want to remain in the light that so easily becomes obscured by our fear and mistrust.

Jesus didn't ask us to like our enemies or to approve of their actions toward us or toward others. He asked us to love them. Love means that we accept people the way they are. We see how they go into fear and push love away and we feel compassion for them. We keep our hearts open to these people. We pray for them. We wish them well.

We can love other people without agreeing with them. In fact, that is one of the ways we can tell if we are loving someone unconditionally. When our acceptance and our love for a person abide even when we disagree with what s/he says or does, we know that we love that person without conditions.

Jesus asked us to love people unconditionally. He didn't say "love only holy people." He said "love everyone." In fact, he anticipated our question: "Do I have to love the person who just attacked me and my family?" He told us clearly and without exception, "Love your enemies."

If you accept your enemies and see them in the light, nothing can take your peace away. Jesus called us to the most difficult task, because he knew that nothing else would release us from the cycle of violence.

part
6

*staying
in your
own life*

Dropping Expectations

No matter how much we plan, prepare and try to control what happens, we cannot always obtain the outcome we want. Life often shows up differently from the way we expect it to.

If we want to embrace life as it is, we need to let our expectations go and deal as gracefully as we can with the reality at hand. That means that we are going to have to make constant mental adjustments each day, each week, and each year that we live.

Imagine that you are sailing on the ocean. To move toward your destination, you must deal with every change in the wind's speed or direction. You can set your course, but you will need to correct for changes in wind and weather. When storms come in, you may need to go out of your way to find safe refuge in the nearest harbor.

Is your life really any different? Are your thoughts and emotions more steady and predictable than the weather? How about the thoughts and feelings of the people you live with?

Life is a serious adventure. Go to sleep at the helm and you could capsize at any moment.

A sailor who does not respect the power of the sea is soon a soggy sailor. If you want to sail through your life, you must respect the power of its changing weather. If you continue to expect a calm, sunny day with a gentle breeze, you won't be prepared to meet the squalls and tempests that unexpectedly blow your way.

Unless you plan to limit your sailing to a few days per year, you had better realize that change and challenge are the rules, not the exceptions. Sometimes, life can be clear sailing, but just as often it's a foggy groping for direction or an unpredictably rough ride in a strong gale.

Let's be realistic. If you think that weathering the lower depths of consciousness—your anxieties, fears, disappointments and unmet expectations (as well as those of the people you care about)—is easy, then you are probably high on some recreational drug or you have a very serious case of denial.

It isn't easy to face your fears. Jesus spent forty days in the desert facing his fears, and I don't think he viewed it as a pleasant experience. But, it was a necessary one. Everyone is tested. Life didn't show up in such an appealing disguise for Job either!

So suffering is a given. That's the realization that Buddha came to. Suffering happens when we don't get something that we want or when we have it and we lose it. Buddha knew that our suffering would not end until we could give up wanting what was unavailable and learn to embrace "what is."

Buddha knew about mental adjustments. He knew that it was our grasping, egotistical mind that needed to relax if our suffering was to end.

All the enlightened ones know this. We are the ones who make the chains that hold us prisoner and we are the ones who unlock the chains. It all happens in consciousness. It all depends on whether we react to our fears or learn to hold them in a compassionate way. It all depends on whether we hold onto our judgments and expectations or whether we release them.

No one goes sailing with a fixed rudder and no one should attempt to go through life with a fixed mind. Our minds must learn to be flexible. We need to move with the flow of water and wind, and not against them.

Flexibility in the moment and patience with the journey are necessary to stay on course. But how do you develop that kind of patience and flexibility?

In the middle of the steam, you run into a large rock or a tree limb and you navigate around it. You learn to go around the obstacles in your life. You back off or, if you see an unexpected opening, you move ahead with confidence. You see what the situation asks from you and you respond to it in the best way you can. You make mistakes and learn from them. You learn to trust the river and respect it at the same time.

Life is a dance between what you expect and what happens. In the process of living, many adjustments are required of you. Are you willing to accept changing weather as a reality of life, or are you looking for still waters?

The ideal cannot manifest until the practical daily reality is accepted. If happiness is the ideal, then we must learn to be happy under all conditions, not just under the conditions we expect or approve.

As long as there is some part of our life that we are unwilling to accept, we will suffer. The neurotic habit of mind that invades our peace more than any other is our need to have something be different than it is.

Acceptance

Asking our lives to be other than they are is like swimming upstream against the current. It doesn't matter how stubborn or strong we are, we will be defeated in the end. No one wins who swims against the tide. The river is bigger than we are. The Tao is greater than our capacity to interfere with it or control it.

Our surrender is guaranteed. The only thing in question is how long we will take to finally accept life as it is. Some of us are more stubborn and less sensitive to pain than others.

The practice of acceptance helps us to affirm life as it unfolds and to take responsibility for making adjustments in our attitude when life shows up differently than we expect it to. To practice acceptance authentically, we must also accept our frustration and our disappointment.

We don't try to change what's happening, nor do we try to change how we are thinking and feeling about it. We just let everything be as it is.

Acceptance is a life raft in the swirling waters of our denial. It allows us to be fully present for life, to move out of the swirling waters and float downstream. Acceptance lifts us up. It keeps our heads above the water so we can navigate to safe ground.

Without acceptance practice, life is often a dangerous place to be. And, even when it is not dangerous, it certainly isn't very much fun.

PRACTICE 11
NOT FINDING FAULT

Today, accept each event, circumstance and interaction with other people just the way it unfolds. Don't make it good or bad, right or wrong. Just be neutral. Just let it be.

If you resist what happens or find fault with it, just be aware of your resistance. Don't make it bad or wrong. Just notice "I am resisting this."

Today, notice the interpretations you make about what happens and set those interpretations aside. Don't become lost in your opinions or those of others. Don't worry about what something means. Just let it be.

Keep saying to yourself "This is okay the way it is. I don't have to find fault with it. I don't have to try to change it or fix it." Today, notice your resistance, take a deep breath, exhale consciously, and let life unfold as it will.

Today, accept everything that comes to you. Let acceptance become a part of your life throughout the day. When the water gets choppy, let your acceptance be the life-raft that takes you through all the twists and turns of the river. Today, breathe and accept what happens and you will meet life respectfully and without fear.

Learning from the Past

When we learn from our mistakes, we know that the past cannot repeat itself. So there's no reason to fear the future. Our hearts can remain open.

When we don't learn from our mistakes, we drag the past around with us. We continue to believe that other people bring suffering upon us.

It's as if we stand in the middle of the road wearing a sign that says "Don't hit me; I'm wounded" and can't understand why people come by and whack us.

When someone suggests to us that we "let go of the past," we look at them mystified. The idea just doesn't register with us, because the past is where we live. It is our identity.

Ironically, if we had the courage to drop the past, we would have a moment that is totally fresh and new, a moment in which we could stop being a victim and exercise the freedom to choose what we want.

Instead of blaming others for the failures of the past, we could begin to take responsibility for our choices in the present moment. That would get us off the merry-go-round of shame and blame and help us plant our feet firmly on the ground.

We might still fail to achieve our goals, but we wouldn't waste our time trying to make someone else responsible for our failure. Instead, we would step back and look honestly and courageously at what happened. We would see our mistake, feel compassion for ourselves and resolve to pay more attention next time.

We would become active learners, instead of passive victims. Because we would take the time to acknowledge and correct our mistakes, we wouldn't have to keep rehearsing the whole operatic performance ad infinitum.

Staying in your own Life

If you don't like starring in one of those melodramatic Italian operas, at the end of which everyone dies, don't try to be responsible for someone else's life and don't let anyone else try to be responsible for yours. Don't try to parent your adult friends or lovers and don't let them try to parent you. Let them take responsibility for their own lives. Let them make their own mistakes and learn from them.

Don't interfere in other people's lives. Don't let others interfere in your life. Bad boundaries here result in a lot of wasted time and energy; they often involve hurt feelings on both sides. Please, step back and look at the line that has been crossed. Step out of other people's lives and back into your own. Ask others to do the same for you.

The interpersonal journey is a hornet's nest when proper boundaries between self and other are not observed. Remember, you are responsible for what you think, feel and experience, and others are responsible for what they think, feel and experience. That's it.

Accept anything else as the truth and you invite trespass or abuse. Don't pour the water into the jar without using this sieve. You'll let end up with water you can't drink.

PRACTICE 12
RESPECTING APPROPRIATE
BOUNDARIES

Today, practice having good boundaries with other people, including the people you live with. Take responsibility for what you think, feel and experience, and ask others to take responsibility for what their experience is.

Be aware when you step over the line and start giving other people advice about how to live their lives. Be aware when you try to analyze, improve or fix other people. Be aware when you think your experience is shared by others or should be. And back off. Let people have their own experience. Respect the thoughts and feelings of others, even when you don't share them or agree with them.

Today, ask people to accept you as you are and refrain from trying to reform you or make you fit their pictures of reality. Don't let other people dictate to you or make decisions for you. Claim your own life today.

Don't give your power away. Don't try to take power away from others. Be in your life and let others be in their lives. Give respect to others and ask for respect in return. Practice good boundaries today.

Don't take responsibility for what someone else thinks, feels or does. Don't try to make anyone else responsible for what you think, feel or do. Own your experience and ask others to own theirs.

When good boundaries are practiced, interactions between people are not difficult. Each person feels accepted and respected. However, when boundaries are compromised, relationships become difficult if not impossible. People feel violated, disrespected, and invalidated.

It's no one's Fault

It's not your fault that things don't work out with other people. When you allow your friends to have their own experience and make their own decisions and they choose to leave, there is nothing that you can do. Other people must make the choices that best honor themselves and so must you.

It's hard to let go of people you have been close to emotionally: parents, children, lovers, friends, workmates. Attachments don't die easily. Realize this and be gentle with yourself. Let yourself mourn the loss. If you really allow yourself to feel your feelings, you will move through them. You won't wallow in your pain or make an identity out of being wounded or rejected.

Relationships with others begin and end. Some last for a lifetime; others for years, months, or weeks. There are no guarantees how long any given relationship will last.

An enlightened person doesn't ask for guarantees. S/he makes a commitment here and now. If the relationship thrives, it is usually because this present-oriented commitment continues to be made by both parties.

No relationship stays in one place emotionally. Each one has its ups and downs. Sometimes the river is calm. Sometimes it is like a roller-coaster. An enlightened person deals with what is happening now. S/he doesn't fantasize about some ideal that isn't being realized. S/he doesn't expect the relationship to be different than it is.

An enlightened person doesn't need to be right or to make the other person wrong. S/he just needs to be honest with herself and others. S/he tells the truth without making the other person wrong.

An enlightened person remembers the light in herself and the light in the other person. Even when s/he forgets, s/he remembers. Her ability to stay in truth may be far from perfect, but her willingness to abandon falsehood as soon as s/he sees it is outstanding.

PRACTICE 13
GRIEVING AND LETTING GO

Today, allow yourself to mourn your emotional losses. Let your sadness and disappointment come up. Feel your pain and allow your tears to flow from your heart.

Remember that you and the other person did the best that you could with the consciousness you had at the time. Forgive yourself for what you could not do. Forgive the other person for what s/he could not do. Today, be thankful for the blessings your relationship brought to you and be glad that your struggle is over.

Be gentle with yourself. Be kind to yourself. If you are hurting, don't be afraid to ask for love and support from others.

Don't blame yourself or the other person. See the light in each of you and hold onto the light. Hold onto the blessing, and let everything else go.

Do this as often as you need to. Don't worry about how long it takes or how many times you do it. Let your heart cry its tears without shutting down. Let your heart be open even though it is pain you are feeling. Feel your love and the love of others through your pain. Let your heart find its own healing.

How you Meet Life

Only your ability to live each day fully prepares you to experience the ups and downs of life without attachment to the outcome. Although you can't control what happens in your life, you can decide how you want to respond to it.

Life is not just something that happens to you. You are not a passive victim here. You are a person with continual choices about how you respond to each event and circumstance of your life. You can respond with strength and dignity or with fear and blame.

How you meet life determines your experience here just as much as the objective content of the experience. Indeed, your life experience is made up of both "what happens to you" and "how you perceive it and respond to it." The objective and subjective content run together.

If you are unwilling to take responsibility for the subjective portion of your experience, you deny your partnership with life. You reject your co-creative power and accept the role of victim. Then, you can blame God or other people for the fact that your experience doesn't meet your expectations.

In other words, you can pretend that how you respond to events is irrelevant and that what happens to you is someone else's responsibility. That's the ultimate cop-out. You deny the very reason why you are here: to awaken from self-created suffering.

Suffering happens when you resist or deny your experience. It happens when you think and feel in a negative, self-pitying way about the events and circumstances of your life. It happens when you try to make something or someone outside of you responsible for the quality of your life.

Learning to move out of this kind of victim-consciousness is the first step on the spiritual path. Until you are willing to take some kind of responsibility for your experience, you cannot know your own creative power. However, when you know that your thoughts and feelings can shape your life, you can begin to have an impact on any situation that you face.

part
7

the heart
of
healing

Responsibility not Guilt

Some New Age writers have confused a lot of people about the subject of responsibility. "You gave yourself cancer," they say and "you can heal it if you are willing."

First of all, the small "you" that is scared and baffled by the predicament you find yourself in did not give you cancer or any other illness. If there is a giver of illness residing in your consciousness it is the transcendent "you" that represents your soul. The gift comes from your soul as a healing crisis. It insists that you wake up and remember your purpose in this embodiment. It is the spiritual "you" addressing the worldly "you" that has become lost in the egoic struggle for survival, name and fame.

Healing comes from the place where you feel safe, loved, and cared for. It is not a race to the finish line or a badge of spiritual correctness. However, New Age terms get carelessly bandied about and, before you know it, people are using phrases like "you can heal yourself" to beat themselves up or to attack other people. The assumption is that if you can't cure yourself of cancer, then you must not be "spiritual." You are a failure, a low life. You don't meditate long enough. Your thoughts are not "spiritually correct."

So there you have it—an idea meant to empower becomes a tool for putting people down. It just goes to show you how any concept can be distorted.

What is healing, after all? Healing means coming home to truth. It means recognizing your true nature. It means bringing the worldly "you" and the transcendent "you" together. It is about integrating your dark side with your light side, your human frailty with your divine origin. Healing means reconciliation, within and without. It means restoring wholeness.

And, like it or not, you can heal and still die from an illness. Death is not a reflection of failure. It can be the epitome of acceptance and understanding. To die at peace, cradled in the arms of love, is as healing as it gets.

Let's not judge illness harshly. Let's not pronounce sentence on ourselves before we look into what's happening.

Since God does not punish us, what is the message of this illness? What is our soul trying to say to us? What is it asking us to transform? Where is it directing our love to go?

For God's sake, don't see your illness as a punishment for being bad. And don't feel that you are spiritually inept if you don't "dematerialize" your illness with the right visualizations, affirmations or prayers.

Pain is a messenger. As you open to your own pain, you discover the message it brings. Then, once you have received the message, you become responsible for it and your treatment options become clear.

You are the healer; not the little, scared "you," trembling in your boots, but the vast, expansive "you" that is one with God. The "you" that knows ministers to the "you" that doesn't. The "you" that loves unconditionally ministers to the "you" that is frozen in the grip of fear.

THE HEART OF HEALING

Where the two "yous" meet, ego surrenders and Christ is born. From then on, death can have no victory, because the temporal has become fused with the eternal. The small self, Atman, has become the great Self, Brahman.

This is the journey that each soul takes. When we look at illness in this light, the only responsibility we have is to hold everyone blameless and to stop withholding our love. In so doing, we go beyond our limited words and concepts into the very heart of healing.

Broken vs. Unbroken

When we get sick, it's hard to realize that there is nothing "wrong" with us. We aren't bad for getting sick, nor is getting sick a punishment for something we did wrong.

Getting sick is just an opportunity to love ourselves more deeply than we ever have before. When we get sick, business as usual comes to a halt. We can't just keep going to the office, or keep taking care of others at home. Now, we have to rest. Now, we have to learn to take care of ourselves.

Our attention turns inward. We begin to tune into how we feel and what we want. The emotional and spiritual dimensions of life become prominent. For the first time in years, perhaps, we ask big questions like "Why am I here?" or "What is my purpose?" or "Where is my soulmate?"

Getting sick prevents us from living in denial any longer. We have to pay attention to our illness. We have to pay attention to our feelings, our hopes, our dreams, our aspirations.

When we get sick, we can no longer live our lives through or for someone else. We cannot sacrifice any more. We need to take ourselves seriously.

So getting sick is a wake up call. It says "Stop living in denial." It says "The old game is over. This may be the only day you have. How do you want to spend it?"

So maybe you want to know: if you had paid more attention to yourself earlier could you have avoided this illness? Perhaps. Perhaps not. Either way, it's time for a change.

It's time to honor yourself fully. Time to be your full creative self. Time to have the intimacy you want. Time for the hugs and gratitudes to be given and received.

No more procrastination.

We cannot put any of this off until tomorrow, for tomorrow may not come. "Now" is the only time we have.

It's a bit ironic but it takes illness (the perception that's something is wrong with us) to help us see that nothing is wrong with us. Our discomfort and "dis-ease" often result from our tendency to try to be someone or something that we are not.

Illness shows us how we are betraying our true self. And its message is quite simple: "That's enough. You can stop doing that now."

Illness says "have the courage and the faith to be yourself."

When we do, healing happens on some level. It may or may not result in the healing of our physical bodies. However, it often results in our healing mentally and emotionally.

Illness seems to be an assault on our wholeness, but it is not. Rather, illness is an assault on that which interferes with or compromises our wholeness.

As such, its purpose is not to punish, but to correct. It exposes untruth so that the truth can be seen. It shows us the torn and scattered to help us find a deeper integration and wholeness.

PRACTICE 14
FINDING YOUR WHOLENESS

Today, realize that you are not your illness. Another way of saying this is "your body may be manifesting illness, but you in your essence are not ill." Somewhere in your heart of hearts is a person who is not broken, a being who is well, whole and at peace.

Today, find that wholeness in yourself. Find the place where you are not broken. Go as deep as you need to go to find that centered, healthy you, the you that is not limited to this body or to this time and space. Find the place within where you know without question that you are loved and accepted just the way you are. And let that "whole you" hold the "broken you." Let the "loved you" hold the one who is not feeling loved.

Healing happens in the place where we feel safe, where we feel accepted, where we feel loved. That is the sanctuary. That is the real hospital.

Find this sanctuary within yourself. Recognize it in the core of your being. You will need to come here many times to remember the truth of who you are. You will have to lay down the burdens of the world and enter this sacred place with empty hands.

Here you are worthy just the way you are. You don't have to "perform" to get a ticket to this place. You don't even need to have a "good diagnosis." Come here when you have run out of medicines and therapies; come even when you have lost hope.

Come here and hold your illness compassionately. Learn to commune with it and hear the message it brings.

Here, even the most terrifying fear can be held in the gentle hands of love. Here you are free to feel whatever you are feeling. Here you are safe to be yourself.

The Inner Sanctuary

It is not just illness that prompts us to seek refuge in the inner temple. It is the trajectory of a life lived in betrayal of self or in the search for the approval of others.

Life isn't always lived on course. Try as we may to honor ourselves and others, we sometimes get lost in unexpected detours and cul de sacs. We all make mistakes. We aren't perfect. No, not even close. At times, we live away from our own truth and we lure others away from theirs. We stop listening to our own guidance and are seduced by sirens.

It's okay to stray from the path. That is certainly part of what makes the journey interesting. But we need a way of getting back on track in our lives. We need to remember to listen for the truth within our own hearts and to honor the truth within others.

Each day, the inner sanctuary awaits our visit. But how many times do we enter? How many times do we stop the incessant pace of our lives long enough to breathe, never mind listen?

For some people, daily meditation takes them into the inner sanctuary. For others, it's a long walk in the woods after dinner. The form doesn't matter as much as the content.

How do you enter the silence of your heart on a daily basis? How do you take time to center and listen?

Without this type of daily ritual, it is hard to stay in touch with the place of healing within. It is hard to rest in your wholeness and stay on course in your life.

PRACTICE 15
GETTING QUIET AND LISTENING

Today, take fifteen minutes at the beginning or at the end of your day to get quiet and listen. Create a simple ritual. Light a candle or some incense. Become aware of your breathing and rest in your heart. Find the place within where there are no judgments about you or anyone else. Find the place of peace and wholeness. And rest there. Listen there. Reconnect with yourself. Join with the essence of others. Let your mind and body be still and let your Spirit rejuvenate. Feel the love that lies at the core of your being and let it extend throughout your body/mind until you feel completely infused and surrounded by it. Breathe and be the presence of love. Breathe and be.

Do this at approximately the same time each day so that it becomes automatic, just as sleeping or eating or exercising becomes automatic. Go within the silence each day. Spend some time remembering who you are and connecting with the truth of your being.

The more this ritual becomes established in your life, the easier it becomes to get quiet periodically throughout the day when you find yourself getting upset or off-center. Just take a deep breath and find the place where you are loved and safe.

It's not hard, because you have been practicing it every day.

And so your practice becomes integrated in your life. Just by watching you, people understand how to go into the Silence. You become the teaching.

Waking Up

Anything can be a wake-up call. You can get cancer, have an emotional breakdown, leave or be abandoned by a partner, experience the death of a loved one, hit bottom from drug or alcohol addiction, get caught for committing a crime. You name it. Anything that turns your life upside down and prevents you from living unconsciously or on automatic pilot can be a wake-up call.

While it may be helpful to have a rhythm in your life, there are times when life becomes too predictable. You aren't being challenged any more. You aren't growing in your capacity to love yourself or others. There's an inner yearning for creative expression and intimacy with others that isn't being satisfied. Indeed, it often seems as if you have built a prison around yourself and thrown away the key. When you feel powerless to change your life, the shadow (unconscious) side goes into motion. Maybe you leave your forty-year marriage and run away with your son's babysitter, or you give up your position as chairman of the board to become a stock car driver.

Energy leaps out of the body it has been trapped in for thirty years. Repression may please the gatekeepers of polite society but it reeks havoc on the imprisoned spirit. Spirit requires continual

ENLIGHTENMENT FOR EVERYONE

growth and transformation. When things become old hat, it needs to find a new hat. It needs to keep expanding and taking risks. Like a hermit crab, it leaves a small, tight shell for a bigger one that permits further growth.

When one person experiences a wake-up call, everyone around him is touched. His wife, his children, his employer, and his community may all be affected. If the people and institutions around him are flexible, they may find a way to accommodate his new growth. If not, he may have to change the nature of his association with them. Often, he will need to leave many of his old roles and responsibilities behind.

If you are facing such a transition, be as gentle as you can with yourself and others. Do not berate yourself because you need to make a change in your life, but don't abandon others either. Communicate what you want and you need. Let people know that you care about them. Redefine your relationships so that they can be mutually supporting. Make amends where they are called for. Say goodbyes when you need to. Transitions are difficult times, but if you can approach them with an open and honest heart, they can open the door to growth and healing for all the people involved.

108

part
8

dancing
souls

Relationship as a Spiritual Path

Perhaps the most intense spiritual practice available to us today is the practice of being in conscious relationship with another person. No other practice goes so quickly to the heart of the matter. No other practice brings our deepest fears to the surface so that we can be aware of them and work through them. Whatever feelings of unworthiness or lack of love may exist in our psyches will be brought into vivid view by the partner who shares our life and our bed.

When we don't feel loved, we reach for the whole assortment of defense mechanisms and emotional armor that we have gathered around us to protect us from emotional abandonment or smothering. Anticipating that someone will leave us or violate our boundaries, we all have ingenious methods of numbing down, dissociating, fighting back or running away.

All of us want the same basic thing. We want to be loved and accepted just the way we are. We don't want to have to change or improve ourselves to meet someone else's standards or expectations.

We think that we need someone with the same interests, the same values, the same temperament, the same upbringing, the same—well, you name it. But then, when we find someone who meets most or all of these criteria, the same thing happens that happened with all the other people who came into our lives. We feel trespassed on or we feel abandoned and we go numb or ballistic.

Is this the inevitable end of story? Perhaps. Those who seek the Madison Avenue image of bliss in relationship are bound to be disappointed. Those who think that it's just a matter of meeting "the right person" are in for a bit of a surprise. If you are scared of giving or receiving love, it doesn't take long before "Mr. or Ms. Right" becomes "Mr. or Ms. Wrong."

If you aren't the "right" person, meeting the "right" person isn't going to do you any good. You have to be for someone else all that you want him or her to be for you before meeting the "right" person has any significance. And that isn't easy when you are terrified of opening up your heart to someone.

If you have to have your soulmate served up to you on a silver platter, better head for the next dining room. On planet earth, love is not served up to you the way you like it.

Love is served up to you with a surgeon's precision. You always meet a partner who has the same level of fear of intimacy that you have. In that sense, you always get a perfect match.

Of course, that doesn't mean that you are going to like what you see in the mirror!

Some of us don't get the message right away, so we keep going out into the collective shopping mall with a sign that says "I'm looking for a woman or a man who isn't full of rage." And who do you think applies for the position?

Have your ever seen those personal ads that say looking for "someone who doesn't play games"? Evidently the people who write these ads keep attracting people who play games into their lives. I guess they don't realize that the only people who respond to an ad like that is someone who wants to play games.

It's a bit of an old story. You are going to attract what you are. There's no way around it.

So, sooner or later, you realize that path of relationship does not take you off into the sunset riding a white steed with your beloved riding radiantly behind you, unless of course that is what you do every day on your own. There are very few surprises—romantic or otherwise—in relationship. Whoever you are is what you get.

Are you tired of looking in the mirror yet?

I have a simple remedy. If you don't want to look at yourself any more, check out the Appalachian trail or that cave in the Himalayas! There are a lot of people walking and meditating in the woods who realized that relationship was not going to be their favorite cup of tea.

Or realize that being in relationship is the fastest and most comprehensive way of meeting yourself (Notice that I didn't say your "soulmate."). I assure you that three weeks in the hot tub with the same person brings as much if not more enlightenment than three months in a Himalayan cave.

The question, of course is, do you want to be enlightened? Or another version of the same question: do you want to meet yourself?

The search for the soulmate or the beloved will always bring you to this doorway, for the beloved is just the mirror image of yourself. When you can love and accept yourself fully, you can embrace the beloved. And not until!

So look slowly and carefully into the mirror. When you look into the beloved's eyes, know that you are looking into your own. When the beloved responds to you in fear, know that it is your fear as well as his or hers. On the path of relationship, there are no more secrets. Everything that was hidden comes out into plain view.

If you don't want to empty your pockets, don't go into relationship. Relationship will strip you of everything that you have. It will take your money, your clothes, your armor and the anger that lies behind it.

If you don't want to get naked, don't go into relationship.

In the old days, people used to go into relationships to hide. And some folks succeeded in hiding from each other for thirty, forty, even fifty years. But those were the old days.

Now, it takes only three years before you and your partner are totally naked, like Adam and Eve when they were kicked out of the garden.

Only this time, don't reach for the loin cloth. Just stand there naked and look into each other's eyes. Let yourself see and be seen. Be vulnerable together. Be afraid together. Let the body shake from its pain and its grief as you hold each other. That is the true garden where you come face to face with the beloved.

There is no more going to sleep here. It is a conscious business. You may not know if you are looking into your eyes or the beloved's eyes, but it doesn't matter any more. They are the same eyes.

Relationship becomes a spiritual path when you and your partner choose to look into the mirror you bring to each other. It means that you need to let the white horse go riderless into the sunset. The person who stands before you is not your savior, but the one who holds your hand while you claim your own salvation.

Are you willing to let the fantasy go and take the hand that reaches out to you? If not, better look for that mountain cave fast before you spot Mr. or Ms. Right getting on the next circular ride. Because once you do, you'll be busy for a while.

Is relationship your spiritual path? If not, what are you doing in relationship?

In the old days, one person would go follow some guru while the other person stayed home. But those were the old days. These days, the only gurus who haven't slept with their disciples are the ones that nobody wants to follow. So you might as well stay home.

Oftentimes I hear people say (usually it is women talking about their husbands) "He isn't spiritual." And I often say "Well, I never met anyone who isn't spiritual! Why don't you give the guy a break…maybe he just expresses his spirituality differently from the way you express yours!"

But then some people have trouble giving up their fantasies. It's just that their fantasy isn't the Marlboro Man riding off into the sunset. It's the yogi or the psychotherapist or the charismatic teacher. We keep forgetting that every generation—indeed every subculture—has its own version of the Marlboro Man.

Fantasies are interesting from a cultural perspective, but they don't help us awaken until we recognize their total improbability. Very few women and men make their living modeling for Playboy or Playgirl. The vast majority of people have a far less homogenous exterior.

Not that there is such a thing as "the average" woman or man, but most women and men have bumps in inauspicious places. They don't have to worry about someone falling in love with their packaging. That's a good thing.

The great gift of intimacy is the removal of the packaging. Intimacy doesn't begin until people look into each other's eyes and see what's really there. It doesn't begin until the Marlboro Man falls off his horse or loses his erection.

If you aren't in a spiritual relationship, then what kind of relationship are you in? Unless you are taking off for that mountain cave, you will find that it's pretty hard to be on a spiritual path if your relationship isn't part of it. That doesn't mean that you and your partner both have to be Baptists or Buddhists. But it does mean that the wrapper must come off with the loin cloth. You cannot live together and not see each other.

That used to be an option, but it isn't any more. Now, the only kind of relationship possible for those who are on a spiritual path is one that is heart to heart and eye to eye. It's a place where all of you becomes visible, vulnerable and self-disclosed. It is a place where boundaries are honored so that they can be negotiated without fear. It is a place where wounds are healed and secrets are revealed. A place of surrender, and yes, ultimately, a place of bliss.

PRACTICE 16
ACCEPTING YOUR PARTNER
AS S/HE IS

Today, your spiritual practice is to accept your partner just as s/he is. No matter what your partner says or does, you are to accept it as gracefully as you can. If s/he crashes the car or spills the tomato sauce on the carpet, you are not to fuss about it. You are not to yell, criticize or complain. You are not to be sarcastic. You are not to reference the past (ie. This is the fourth time this month that you have "smashed the car" or "spilled the sauce.") You are to simply accept it in stride and act as if everything is fine. Moreover, reassure your partner that you love him or her. Ask if there is anything you can do to make his or her life easier.

Today, let nothing interfere with your love for your partner. Put your partner first and let everything else come afterward. Perhaps it would help you to pretend that you are courting your partner again. You want to please. You want to make a good impression. You want your partner to feel that you are an outstanding and attentive lover.

If it's hard for you to do this, just be aware of it. Maybe you've become a little rusty in the courting department. Put some grease on the wheel and keep at it. You'll get better. You might even begin to remember why you fell in love with him or her to begin with. If so, use those memories to motivate you to do your very best. Give your partner all the love and acceptance you have to give. Don't hold anything back.

Do this at least one day a week. Just pick a day and do it. Maybe your partner will catch on. Perhaps s/he'll say, "I don't know what comes over you on Thursdays" or "can we talk on Thursday?" Then, you know that it's working. Make this your private Sabbath ritual. Once a week, fall in love again. Serve your partner. Listen with understanding. Accept what happens. Be grateful for your partner's presence in your life.

If you are reading this book with your partner, each of you can pick a different day. Then, twice a week, your relationship will be receiving an important healing that will help you maintain your intimacy and trust. Try it and you'll see.

Nurturing Your Partnership

In order to love another person, you must take time to know and be with that person. You cannot fit the beloved in between work, chores and children. The beloved needs his or her own time.

Do you take time to do something thoughtful for your partner? Do you take time to listen, support and connect? Do you take time to do something with your partner that you both enjoy?

When you don't take time to nurture your partnership, the relationship goes hungry. Impatience, judgment and distrust set in. Communication gets sloppy. Inner temperatures rise and conflicts begin to brew.

Partnership cannot be a secondary thing. It can't come after work or other responsibilities. It must come first.

If you choose to be in relationship, your responsibility to connect with your partner becomes as important as your responsibility to connect with your inner self. You cannot deny one for the sake of the other. They are equally important.

PRACTICE 17
DAILY CLEARING AND COMMUNION

If you want to maintain true intimacy in your relationship, take some time every day to clear and commune with your partner. Pick a time towards the end of the day that works for you and stick to it, but don't choose a time when one or both of you will be too tired to do this practice.

Sit facing your partner with your eyes closed. (You can hold hands if you want to.) Do some deep breathing to relax and continue breathing in and out of your abdomen whenever you need to. Open your eyes and look into your partner's eyes. Hold this eye contact as long as it feels comfortable—anywhere from 10 to 30 seconds is probably about right for the first time. Then close your eyes again and open them when you are ready to look into your partner's eyes again. If you open your eyes first, wait for your partner's eyes to open and then hold this eye contact a little longer than the last time. Do this several times until you feel emotionally connected to your partner.

Then, while looking at your partner, see if there is anything that you need to communicate to him or her. Perhaps s/he made a remark earlier that day that angered you or hurt your feelings. Maybe you did not feel heard, appreciated, or understood. Let any feelings of emotional disturbance or distance come up for you.

Then tell your partner "I'm feeling a little shut down now because
...... or "I was feeling a little distant from you earlier today
because ......" Say what you have to say in a gentle, non-blaming
way to your partner. Put the emphasis on how you felt, not on
what your partner did or did not do. Make your communication
about you and what interfered with your feeling fully connected
to your partner and not about what might have been going on for
your partner. That's not your concern right now.

When listening to your partner's sharing, accept what s/he
says at face value. Don't try to explain your actions or defend
yourself. Just listen and accept. Don't cross examine your partner or make him or her justify how s/he feels. Don't respond to
what your partner is saying. Just listen. You don't have to
change your behavior or fix anything. You don't have to make
your partner feel better. Just hear what is being said and learn
something about your partner. This information will be very
valuable to you if you can receive it. Be silent and hold a loving,
accepting space while your partner talks. If your partner says
something that is hard for you to hear, take a deep breath into
your abdomen. Come back into your heart. Look into your
partner's eyes. Stay in communion.

When your partner is done speaking, take a minute or two of
silence and then switch. See if you have any hurt or angry feelings you have been holding onto. See if there is something you
have been wanting to say but have not said yet to your partner.
Get in touch with where you are tensing up or holding back.

Remember to make it about you, not about your partner. Say "I was feeling disconnected or distant from you when ......" Emphasize what was happening for you. Use whatever words come to you. You don't have to wait for the perfect words. And don't look to your partner anticipating a response. You are not looking for a solution to anything here. You are just saying where you feel strained, distant or disconnected. You can also share when you felt really close and connected to your partner. Indeed, sharing positive things can make it easier for your partner to hear your feelings of discomfort.

When you are done sharing, tell you partner "I'm done now. Thank you for listening to me." Then look into each other's eyes until you both feel complete, tell each other how much you love and appreciate each other and give each other a hug. Then, you are both clear and can go to bed feeling connected with and responsive to each other.

Do not under any circumstances move into a problem-solving mode during or after completing this exercise. Understand that there is nothing to change or fix right now. Right now, you needed to be heard and you were heard. That's enough. Trust in the power of that communication. It will go to work in your relationship without any direction from you or any agreements with your partner. Its healing energy is immediately brought to bear on the relationship. Just by holding what was shared in a loving, compassionate manner, the process of transformation begins. Learn to trust it. Learn to share what holds you apart and then let it go.

Don't hold onto the problem or the feelings of separation or they will follow you. On the other hand, don't stuff your feelings. Take the time to speak them and clear them. Then your heart will not be heavy. And you and your partner can move back into the joy that you spontaneously create together.

Do this exercise once per day and you will be buying an insurance policy for your relationship. Or more accurately, you will be practicing wellness and preventative medicine.

As an individual, you may find that you need to sit down daily to meditate or get quiet and that this ritual helps to keep you centered and balanced. Your relationship needs a similar ritual to stay centered and balanced. Take the time to clear with your partner, and storms will come and go without doing damage. Seas may rise and winds may blow, but you both know that you can weather any storm because you have taken the time to check in with your gods and demons every day.

Cars need an oil change every 3,000 miles. Relationships need a clearing once per day.

Change the oil every 3,000 miles and you can get 150,000 200,000 miles on your engine. Clear and commune with your partner every day and you can live a life of unmitigated trust and bliss.

Shared Guidance and Experience

In a spiritual relationship, direction comes from the guidance of both people. You no longer make decisions based on what is good for you alone. It has to be good for the other person too.

A spiritual relationship is a "we" space, not an "I" space. You want the other person to be happy and fulfilled as much as you desire happiness and fulfillment for yourself.

Decisions which you used to make alone are now made with your partner. You discuss your guidance and wait for consensus before you make any significant choice that affects both of you.

In a spiritual relationship, there is a balance of power. That is not because your partner demands it or is skilled in negotiating it. Rather, it is a function of the mutual respect you and your partner have for each other.

In a non-spiritual relationship, people either deny their individual needs to meet the partner's needs (become co-dependent) or they insist on meeting their needs at the expense of the partner (become selfish and self-centered). A spiritual partnership by definition requires more than denial or indulgence. Neither narrow, self-interest nor self-sacrifice will do. A spiritual relationship requires that the needs of both people be equally addressed.

If you want to walk through this world together as a couple, don't insist on doing things "your way" or settle for doing things "the other person's way." Look for consensus. Wait for a strategy that honors your needs and your partner's needs equally. Have faith that you can find such a strategy, even if it seems far off or improbable now.

On the other hand, be careful not to seek agreement with your partner at the price of truth. You need to be truthful with each other first and then see what agreements are possible.

Sometimes you may agree to explore a course of action together without knowing if it is entirely the right course of action. If you do this, be very clear with the other person as soon as something does not feel right to you. Don't go further down the wrong road than you need to. Speak up when things are not working. Renegotiate commitments that feel awkward or confining to you.

Living in the space of "we" with your partner is an extraordinary accomplishment. "We" is a space that is as respectful to you as it is to the other person. It is a place of existential equality.

We use the first person plural all the time, but we haven't come close to understanding what it means. "We" cannot and does not mean either self-betrayal or the betrayal of the partner. "We" means honoring both people at the same time. It is a moment to moment proposition. Being equal partners in this moment is spiritual practice. It is a great discipline. Perhaps more than any other path, it can bring you and your partner home.

Retaining the Magic

Don't lose the magic of your love for your partner. You may need to go to the office or do the laundry, but don't forget to take time to look into your partner's eyes when you wake in the morning or go to bed at night. Don't forget the timeless dimension of your experience together.

There is a place in which you and the beloved are joined as one. It lives in your hearts when you are digging in the garden or repairing the rock wall. It is the altar you approached many years ago but have since forgotten. Each day, you must find it. Each day you must find the sacred place in your relationship. When that sacredness is not held by both people, it begins to fall away.

And then time seals the journey with its kiss of death and it is too late for love to bloom. Do not let the mundane tasks of daily life so preoccupy you that you have no time to affirm the love that you and your partner share.

That love is the yoke that binds you as you pull the cart of life together. No other yoke can hold you gently but firmly in place so that the weight of living is evenly distributed between you. No other harness can hold you to each other's pace so that your footsteps move in unison as you travel up the hardest hills to find the sun rising before you in spectacular glory. No other tie can so tether your hearts that they beat together, pull together, yearn, cry, and laugh together as you walk side by side on the journey home.

part
9

*practice
not
practicing*

Practice not Practicing

Most of us do not engage in a regular spiritual practice that can increase our awareness of ourselves and others. We have lots of ideas about what truth is, but we haven't internalized those concepts. We haven't made them a living, breathing part of our lives.

The purpose of the practices suggested in this book is to help us internalize truth so that we can live in a way that honors ourselves and others. The danger in offering a series of practices such as these is that people might think that they must engage in them in order to become enlightened.

That is not what I am suggesting. We engage in spiritual practice for one reason: to remember what we have forgotten. We practice to remember the light inside us and the light inside others.

Spiritual practice is not a searching for something that is lacking, but a re-discovery of what is present in abundance. None of us lack light. We just become very skillful in hiding it with our judgments.

Our spiritual practice does not attempt to add anything to our essential nature. Rather, it seeks to strip away the elaborate masks that we wear, masks that disguise the truth within. It is a process of undoing what is false.

When we look beneath the masks we wear, we encounter our fear. Trying to cover up that fear or push it away doesn't help us see our true nature. Only by accepting our fear and observing it compassionately do we move through it to experience our essence.

When we are no longer afraid of our own fear, it is powerless to take us off-course in our lives. Then, we live with fear as our everyday companion. We walk with it and we dance with it. This is the fruit of a committed, spiritual practice.

Facing our fears, we don't have to project them onto others. We clear the battlefield of its unnecessary carnage. We walk out into the field in the wind and the rain, with lightening flashing and thunder reverberating overhead and, in just minutes, the storm passes over us.

It takes courage to face our fears, but it is the quickest way to self-integration. It is the way that we learn to trust who we are and be authentic with others. Jesus said that we would know the tree by its fruits and so it is. Those who are loving toward others have walked through the dark night of the soul. They have embraced the spark within and nurtured it to become a steady flame. They are on fire and we know it. They cannot hide the warmth and brightness of their love.

PRACTICE 18
NOT PRACTICING

So today, one final practice: today, practice not practicing. Today, there is nothing to do except what you are doing. Today, you are already enlightened right here, right now. If you can do this practice, you can forget the others.

Namaste,

Paul Ferrini

Recommended Reading

In addition to the practices suggested in this book, other spiritual exercises can be found in my books *The Ecstatic Moment*, *Creating a Spiritual Relationship*, and *Living in the Heart*. If you have found this book helpful, you might want to read those books as well. I want to particularly recommend *Living in the Heart* to you. It describes The *Affinity Group Process* in great detail and will help you learn how to facilitate a group. Currently, groups are meeting in a number of cities.

The *Affinity Process* helps us learn how to love unconditionally and begin to build spiritual community at the grass roots level. These groups not only help us to awaken, but they help us bring non-sectarian, non-denominational spiritual practices into our schools, prisons, hospitals, businesses and community agencies. The results are inspiring and transformational.

Notes on the Cover Art

Buddha Under the Mango Tree, by Ch'ên Yung Chih (*circa 1025*) portrays a miracle which the Buddha performed as a preliminary to the Great Miracle of Sravasti. At the command of the Buddha, the gardener Ganda planted a mango seed, whereupon a mango tree sprang up immediately. Almost instantly it was covered with flowers and fruit. Here, the Buddha is depicted holding a mango in his hand.

Paul Ferrini's unique blend of radical Christianity and other wisdom traditions, goes beyond self-help and recovery into the heart of healing. He is the author of twenty-four books including his latest books *I am the Door, Reflections of the Christ Mind* and *The Way of Peace.* His *Christ Mind* Series includes the bestseller *Love Without Conditions, The Silence of the Heart, Miracle of Love* and *Return to the Garden.* Other recent books include *Creating a Spiritual Relationship, Grace Unfolding, Living in the Heart, Crossing the Water, The Ecstatic Moment* and *Illuminations on the Road to Nowhere.*

Paul Ferrini is the founder and editor of *Miracles Magazine* and a nationally known teacher and workshop leader. His conferences, retreats, and Affinity Group Process have helped thousands of people deepen their practice of forgiveness and open their hearts to the divine presence in themselves and others. For more information on Paul's workshops and retreats or The Affinity Group Process, contact Heartways Press, P. O. Box 99, Greenfield, MA 01302-0099 or call 413-774-9474.

BOOKS AND TAPES
AVAILABLE FROM HEARTWAYS PRESS

Paul Ferrini's luminous new translation captures the essence of Lao Tzu and the fundamental aspects of Taoism in a way that no single book ever has!

The Great Way of All Beings:
Renderings of Lao Tzu
by Paul Ferrini
ISBN 1-879159-46-5
320 pages hardcover $23.00

New

The Great Way of All Beings: Renderings of Lao Tzu is composed of two different versions of Lao Tzu's masterful scripture *Tao Te Ching*. Part one, River of Light, is an intuitive, spontaneous rendering of the material that captures the spirit of the *Tao Te Ching*, but does not presume to be a close translation. Part Two is a more conservative translation of the *Tao Te Ching* that attempts as much as possible to stay with the words and images used in the original text. The words and images used in Part One leap out from the center to explore how the wisdom of the Tao touches us today. By contrast, the words and images of Part Two turn inward toward the center, offering a more feminine, receptive version of the material.

"We listen for it, yet its note can't be heard.
We look intently for it, yet its image can't be seen.

Although it has no beginning,
it leads us back to our original nature

Although it has no end,
it helps us come to completion."

A Practical Guide to Realizing your True Nature

*"Enlightenment is the realization of the light that is within you.
It is the conscious recognition and acceptance of that light.
Enlightenment is discovering who you already are and being it fully."*

Enlightenment for Everyone
by Paul Ferrini
ISBN 1-879159-45-7
160 pages hardcover $16.00

Enlightenment is not contingent on finding the right teacher or having some kind of peak spiritual experience. There's nothing that you need to get, find or acquire to be enlightened. You don't need a priest or rabbi to intercede with God for you. You don't need a special technique or meditation practice. You don't need to memorize scripture or engage in esoteric breathing practices. You simply need to discover who you already are and be it fully. This essential guide to self-realization contains eighteen spiritual practices that will enable you to awaken to the truth of your being. This exquisite hardcover book will be a life-long companion and will make an inspirational gift to friends and family.

A comprehensive selection from the Christ Mind teachings just released by Doubleday

New

"*Open yourself now to the wisdom of Jesus, as Paul Ferrini has brought it through. These words can inspire you to greater insights and understandings, to more clarity and a grander resolve to make changes in your life that can truly change the world.*"

Neale Donald Walsch, author of *Conversations with God.*

Reflections of the Christ Mind:
The Present Day Teachings of Jesus
by Paul Ferrini
Introduction by Neale Donald Walsch
ISBN 0-385-49952-3
302 pages hardcover $19.95

Reflections of the Christ Mind contains excerpts from *Love Without Conditions, Silence of the Heart, Miracle of Love* and *Return to the Garden.* It presents the most important teachings in the *Christ Mind* series.

I am the Door

I am the Door
by Paul Ferrini
ISBN 1-879159-41-4
288 pages hardcover $21.95

Years ago, Paul Ferrini began hearing a persistent inner voice that said "I want you to acknowledge me." He also had a series of dreams in which Jesus appeared to teach him. Later, when Ferrini's relationship with his teacher was firmly established, the four books in the Reflections of the Christ Mind series were published. Here, in this lovely lyrical collection, we can hear the voice of Jesus speaking directly to us about practical topics of everyday life that are close to our hearts like work and livelihood, relationships, community, forgiveness, spiritual practices, and miracles. When you put this book down, there will no doubt in your mind that the teachings of the master are alive today. Your life will never be the same.

Taking Back Our Schools
by Paul Ferrini
ISBN 1-879159-43-0 $10.95

This book is written for parents who are concerned about the education of their children. It presents a simple idea that could transform the school system in this country. This book does not pretend to have all the answers. It is the start of a conversation. It is chapter one in a larger book that has not yet been written. If you choose to work with these ideas,you may be one of the authors of the chapters to come.

The Way of Peace
A New System of Spiritual Guidance

Paul Ferrini

The Way of Peace
by Paul Ferrini
ISBN 1-879159-42-2
256 pages hardcover
$19.95

The Way of Peace is a simple method for connecting with the wisdom and truth that lie within our hearts. The two hundred and sixteen oracular messages in this book were culled from the bestselling *Reflections of the Christ Mind* series by Paul Ferrini.

Open this little book spontaneously to receive inspirational guidance, or ask a formal question and follow the simple divinatory procedure described in the introduction. You will be amazed at the depth and the accuracy of the response you receive.

Like the *I-Ching*, the *Book of Runes*, and other systems of guidance, *The Way of Peace* empowers you to connect with peace within and act in harmony with your true self and the unique circumstances of your life.

Special dice, blessed by the author, are available for using *The Way of Peace* as an oracle. To order these dice, send $3.00 plus shipping.

"The Road to Nowhere is the path through your heart. It is not a journey of escape. It is a journey through your pain to end the pain of separation."

Illuminations on the Road to Nowhere
160 pages paperback $12.95
ISBN 1-879159-44-9

There comes a time for all of us when the outer destinations no longer satisfy and we finally understand that the love and happiness we seek cannot be found outside of us. It must be found in our own hearts, on the other side of our pain.

This book makes it clear that we can no longer rely on outer teachers or teachings to find our spiritual identity. Nor can we find who we are in relationships where boundaries are blurred and one person makes decisions for another. If we want to be authentic, we can't allow anyone else to be an authority for us, nor can we allow ourselves to be an authority for another person.

This provocative book challenges many of our basic assumptions about personal happiness and the meaning of our relationship with others and with God.

Our Surrender Invites Grace

Grace Unfolding:
The Art of Living A Surrendered Life
96 pages paperback $9.95
ISBN 1-879159-37-6

As we surrender to the truth of our being, we learn to relinquish the need to control our lives, figure things out, or predict the future. We begin to let go of our judgments and interpretations and accept life the way it is. When we can be fully present with whatever life brings, we are guided to take the next step on our journey. That is the way that grace unfolds in our lives.

The Relationship Book You've Been Waiting For

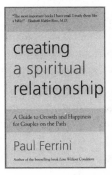

Creating a Spiritual Relationship: A Guide to Growth and Happiness for Couples on the Path
144 pages paperback $10.95
ISBN 1-879159-39-2

This simple but profound guide to growth and happiness for couples will help you and your partner:

* Make a realistic commitment to each other
* Develop a shared experience that nurtures your relationship
* Give each other the space to grow and express yourselves as individuals
* Communicate by listening without judgment and telling the truth in a non-blaming way
* Understand how you mirror each other
* Stop blaming your partner and take responsibility for your thoughts, feelings and actions
* Practice forgiveness together on an ongoing basis

These seven spiritual principles will help you weather the ups and downs of your relationship so that you and your partner can grow together and deepen the intimacy between you. The book also includes a special section on living alone and preparing to be in relationship and a section on separating with love when a relationship needs to change form or come to completion.

Return to the Garden
Reflections of The Christ Mind, Part IV
$12.95, Paperback
ISBN 1-879159-35-X

"In the Garden, all our needs were provided for. We knew no struggle or hardship. We were God's beloved. But happiness was not enough for us. We wanted the freedom to live our own lives. To evolve, we had to learn to become love-givers, not just love-receivers.

We all know what happened then. We were cast out of the Garden and for the first time in our lives we felt shame, jealousy, anger, lack. We experienced highs and lows, joy and sorrow. Our lives became difficult. We had to work hard to survive. We had to make mistakes and learn from them.

Initially, we tried to blame others for our mistakes. But that did not make our lives any easier. It just deepened our pain and misery. We had to learn to face our fears, instead of projecting them onto each other.

Returning to the Garden, we are different than we were when we left hellbent on expressing our creativity at any cost. We return humble and sensitive to the needs of all. We return not just as cre-ated, but as co-creator, not just as son of man, but also as son of God."

Learn the Spiritual Practice
Associated with the Christ Mind Teachings

Living in the Heart The Affinity Process and the Path of Unconditional Love and Acceptance
Paperback $10.95
ISBN 1-879159-36-8

The long awaited, definitive book on the *Affinity Process* is finally here. For years, the *Affinity Process* has been refined by participants so that it could be easily understood and experienced. Now, you can learn how to hold a safe, loving, non-judgmental space for yourself and others which will enable you to open your heart and move through your fears. The *Affinity Process* will help you learn to take responsibility for your fears and judgments so that you won't project them onto others. It will help you learn to listen deeply and without judgment to others. And it will teach you how to tell your truth clearly without blaming others for your experience.

Part One contains an in-depth description of the principles on which the *Affinity Process* is based. Part Two contains a detailed discussion of the *Affinity Group Guidelines*. And Part Three contains a manual for people who wish to facilitate an *Affinity Group* in their community.

If you are a serious student of the *Christ Mind* teachings, this book is essential for you. It will enable you to begin a spiritual practice which will transform your life and the lives of others. It will also offer you a way of extending the teachings of love and forgiveness throughout your community.

Now Finally our Bestselling Title on Audio Tape

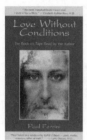

Love Without Conditions,
Reflections of the Christ Mind, Part I

by Paul Ferrini
The Book on Tape Read by the Author
2 Cassettes, Approximately 3.25 hours
ISBN 1-879159-24-4 $19.95

Now on audio tape: the incredible book from Jesus calling us to awaken to our own Christhood. Listen to this gentle, profound book while driving in your car or before going to sleep at night. Elisabeth Kubler-Ross calls this "the most important book I have read. I study it like a Bible." Find out for yourself how this amazing book has helped thousands of people understand the radical teachings of Jesus and begin to integrate these teachings into their lives.

With its heartfelt combination of sensuality and spirituality, Paul Ferrini's poetry has been compared to the poetry of Rumi.

Crossing The Water:
Poems About Healing
and Forgiveness in
Our Relationships

The time for healing and reconciliation has come, Ferrini writes. Our relationships help us heal childhood wounds, walk through our deepest fears, and cross over the water of our emotional pain. Just as the rocks in the river are pounded and caressed to rounded stone, the rough edges of our personalities are worn smooth in the context of a committed relationship. If we can keep our hearts open, we can heal together, experience genuine equality, and discover what it means to give and receive love without conditions.

With its heartfelt combination of sensuality and spirituality, Paul Ferrini's poetry has been compared to the poetry of Rumi. These luminous poems demonstrate why Paul Ferrini is first a poet, a lover and a mystic. Come to this feast of the beloved with an open heart and open ears. 96 pp. paper ISBN 1-879159-25-2 $9.95.

Miracle of Love: Reflections of the Christ Mind, Part III

In this volume of the Christ Mind series, Jesus sets the record straight regarding a number of events in his life. He tells us: "I was born to a simple woman in a barn. She was no more a virgin than your mother was." Moreover, the virgin birth was not the only myth surrounding his life and teaching. So were the concepts of vicarious atonement and physical resurrection.

Relentlessly, the master tears down the rigid dogma and hierarchical teachings that obscure his simple message of love and forgiveness. He encourages us to take him down from the pedestal and the cross and see him as an equal brother who found the way out of suffering by opening his heart totally. We too can open our hearts and find peace and happiness. "The power of love will make miracles in your life as wonderful as any attributed to me," he tells us. "Your birth into this embodiment is no less holy than mine. The love that you extend to others is no less important than the love I extend to you." 192 pp. paper ISBN 1-879159-23-6 $12.95.

The Ecstatic Moment: A Practical Manual for Opening Your Heart and Staying in It.

A simple, power-packed guide that helps us take appropriate responsibility for our experience and establish healthy boundaries with others. Part II contains many helpful exercises and meditations that teach us to stay centered, clear and open in heart and mind. The Affinity Group Process and other group practices help us learn important listening and communication skills that can transform our troubled relationships. Once you have read this book, you will keep it in your briefcase or on your bedside table, referring to it often. You will not find a more practical, down to earth guide to contemporary spirituality. You will want to order copies for all your friends. 128 pp. paper ISBN 1-879159-18-X $10.95

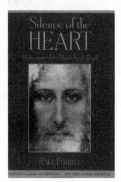

The Silence of the Heart: Reflections of the Christ Mind, Part II

A powerful sequel to Love Without Conditions. John Bradshaw says: "with deep insight and sparkling clarity, this book demonstrates that the roots of all abuse are to be found in our own self-betrayal. Paul Ferrini leads us skillfully and courageously beyond shame, blame, and attachment to our wounds into the depths of self-forgiveness... a must read for all people who are ready to take responsibility for their own healing." 218 pp. paper. ISBN 1-879159-16-3 $14.95

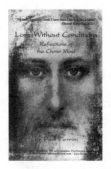

Love Without Conditions: Reflections of the Christ Mind, Part I

An incredible book from Jesus calling us to awaken to our Christhood. Rarely has any book conveyed the teachings of the master in such a simple but profound manner. This book will help you to bring your understanding from the head to the heart so that you can model the teachings of love and forgiveness in your daily life. 192 pp. paper ISBN 1-879159-15-5 $12.00

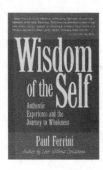

The Wisdom of the Self

This ground-breaking book explores our authentic experience and our journey to wholeness. "Your life is your spiritual path. Don't be quick to abandon it for promises of bigger and better experiences. You are getting exactly the experiences you need to grow. If your growth seems too slow or uneventful for you, it is because you have not fully embraced the situations and relationships at hand...To know the Self is to allow everything, to embrace the totality of who we are, all that we think and feel, all of our fear, all of our love." 229 pp. paper ISBN 1-879159-14-7 $12.00

The Twelve Steps of Forgiveness

A practical manual for healing ourselves and our relationships. This book gives us a step-by-step process for moving through our fears, projections, judgments, and guilt so that we can take responsibility for creating the life we want. With great gentleness, we learn to embrace our lessons and to find equality with others. A must read for all in recovery and others seeking spiritual wholeness. 128 pp. paper ISBN 1-879159-10-4 $10.00

The Wounded Child's Journey: Into Love's Embrace

This book explores a healing process in which we confront our deep-seated guilt and fear, bringing love and forgiveness to the wounded child within. By surrendering our judgments of self and others, we overcome feelings of separation and dismantle co-dependent patterns that restrict our self-expression and ability to give and receive love. 225pp. paper ISBN 1-879159-06-6 $12.00

The Bridge to Reality

A Heart-Centered Approach to *A Course in Miracles* and the Process of Inner Healing. Sharing his experiences of spiritual awakening, Paul emphasizes self-acceptance and forgiveness as cornerstones of spiritual practice. Presented with beautiful photos, this book conveys the essence of The Course as it is lived in daily life. 192 pp. paper ISBN 1-879159-03-1 $12.00

Virtues of The Way

A lyrical work of contemporary scripture reminiscent of the Tao Te Ching. Beautifully illustrated, this inspirational book will help you cultivate the spiritual values required to fulfill your creative purpose and live in harmony with others. 64 pp. paper
ISBN 1-879159-02-3 $7.50

From Ego to Self

108 illustrated affirmations designed to offer you a new way of viewing conflict situations so that you can overcome negative thinking and bring more energy, faith and optimism into your life. 144 pp. paper ISBN 1-879159-01-5 $10.00

The Body of Truth

A crystal clear introduction to the universal teachings of love and forgiveness. This book traces all forms of suffering to negative attitudes and false beliefs, which we have the ability to transform. 64 pp. paper ISBN 1-879159-02-3 $7.50

Available Light

Inspirational, passionate poems dealing with the work of inner integration, love and relationships, death and re-birth, loss and abundance, life purpose and the reality of spiritual vision. 128 pp. paper ISBN 1-879159-05-8 $12.00

Poetry and Guided Meditation Tapes
by Paul Ferrini

The Poetry of the Soul

With its heartfelt combination of sensuality and spirituality, Paul Ferrini's poetry has been compared to the poetry of Rumi. These luminous poems read by the author demonstrate why Paul Ferrini is first a poet, a lover and a mystic. Come to this feast of the beloved with an open heart and open ears. With Suzi Kesler on piano. $10.00 ISBN 1-879159-26-0

The Circle of Healing

The meditation and healing tape that many of you have been seeking. This gentle meditation opens the heart to love's presence and extends that love to all the beings in your experience. A powerful tape with inspirational piano accompaniment by Michael Gray. ISBN 1-879159-08-2 $10.00

Healing the Wounded Child

A potent healing tape that accesses old feelings of pain, fragmentation, self-judgment and separation and brings them into the light of conscious awareness and acceptance. Side two includes a hauntingly beautiful "inner child" reading from The Bridge to Reality with piano accompaniment by Michael Gray. ISBN 1-879159-11-2 $10.00

Forgiveness: Returning to the Original Blessing

A self healing tape that helps us accept and learn from the mistakes we have made in the past. By letting go of our judgments and ending our ego-based search for perfection, we can bring our darkness to the light, dissolving anger, guilt, and shame. Piano accompaniment by Michael Gray. ISBN 1-879159-12-0 $10.00

Paul Ferrini Talks and Workshop Tapes

Answering Our Own Call for Love

Paul tells the story of his own spiritual awakening: his Atheist upbringing, how he began to open to the presence of God, and his connection with Jesus and the Christ Mind teaching. In a very clear, heart-felt way, Paul presents to us the spiritual path of love, acceptance, and forgiveness. 1 Cassette $10.00 ISBN 1-879159-33-3

The Ecstatic Moment

Shows us how we can be with our pain compassionately and learn to nurture the light within ourselves, even when it appears that we are walking through darkness. Discusses subjects such as living in the present, acceptance, not fixing self or others, being with our discomfort and learning that we are lovable as we are. 1 Cassette $10.00 ISBN 1-879159-27-9

Honoring Self and Other

Helps us understand the importance of not betraying ourselves in our relationships with others. Focuses on understanding healthy boundaries, setting limits, and saying no to others in a loving way. Real life examples include a woman who is married to a man who is chronically critical of her, and a gay man who wants to tell his judgmental parents that he has AIDS. 1 Cassette $10.00 ISBN 1-879159-34-1

Seek First the Kingdom

Discusses the words of Jesus in the Sermon on the Mount: "Seek first the kingdom and all else will be added to you." Helps us understand how we create the inner temple by learning to hold our judgments of self and other more compassionately. The love of God flows through our love and acceptance of ourselves. As we establish our connection to the divine within ourselves, we don't need to look outside of ourselves for love and acceptance. Includes fabulous music by The Agape Choir and Band. 1 Cassette $10.00 ISBN 1-879159-30-9

Double Cassette Tape Sets

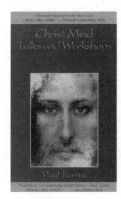

Ending the Betrayal of the Self

A roadmap for integrating the opposing voices in our psyche so that we can experience our own wholeness. Delineates what our responsibility is and isn't in our relationships with others, and helps us learn to set clear, firm, but loving boundaries. Our relationships can become areas of sharing and fulfillment, rather than mutual invitations to co-dependency and self betrayal. 2 Cassettes $16.95 ISBN 1-879159-28-7

Relationships: Changing Past Patterns

Begins with a Christ Mind talk describing the link between learning to love and accept ourselves and learning to love and accept others. Helps us understand how we are invested in the past and continue to replay our old relationship stories. Helps us get clear on what we want and understand how to be faithful to it. By being totally committed to ourselves, we give birth to the beloved within and also without. Includes an in-depth discussion about meditation, awareness, hearing our inner voice, and the Affinity Group Process. 2 Cassettes $16.95 ISBN 1-879159-32-5

Relationship As a Spiritual Path

Explores concrete ways in which we can develop a relationship with ourselves and learn to take responsibility for our own experience, instead of blaming others for our perceived unworthiness. Also discussed: accepting our differences, the new paradigm of relationship, the myth of the perfect partner, telling our truth, compassion vs. rescuing, the unavailable partner, abandonment issues, negotiating needs, when to say no, when to stay and work on a relationship and when to leave. 2 Cassettes $16.95 ISBN 1-879159-29-5

Opening to Christ Consciousness

Begins with a Christ Mind talk giving us a clear picture of how the divine spark dwells within each of us and how we can open up to God-consciousness on a regular basis. Deals with letting go and forgiveness in our relationships with our parents, our children and our partners. A joyful, funny, and scintillating tape you will want to listen to many times. 2 Cassettes $16.95 ISBN 1-879159-31-7

Poster and Notecards

Risen Christ Posters & Notecards
11" x 17"
Poster suitable for framing
ISBN 1-879159-19-8 $10.00

Set of 8 Notecards with Envelopes
ISBN 1-879159-20-1 $10.00

Ecstatic Moment Posters & Notecards

8.5" x 11"
Poster suitable for framing
ISBN 1-879159-21-X $5.00

Set of 8 Notecards with Envelopes
ISBN 1-879159-22-8 $10.00

Heartways Press Order Form

Name _____

Address_____

City _____State _____Zip_____

Phone/Fax_____Email_____

Books by Paul Ferrini

The Great Way of All Beings:
   Renderings of Lao Tzu Hardcover ($23.00)   _____

Enlightenment for Everyone Hardcover ($16.00)   _____

Taking Back Our Schools ($10.95)   _____

The Way of Peace Hardcover ($19.95)   _____

   Way of Peace Dice ($3.00)   _____

Illuminations on the Road to Nowhere ($12.95)   _____

I am the Door Hardcover ($21.95)   _____

Reflections of the Christ Mind: The Present Day
   Teachings of Jesus Hardcover ($19.95)   _____

Creating a Spiritual Relationship ($10.95)   _____

Grace Unfolding: The Art of Living A
   Surrendered Life ($9.95)   _____

Return to the Garden ($12.95)   _____

Living in the Heart ($10.95)   _____

Miracle of Love ($12.95)   _____

Crossing the Water ($9.95)   _____

The Ecstatic Moment ($10.95)   _____

The Silence of the Heart ($14.95)   _____

Love Without Conditions ($12.00)   _____

The Wisdom of the Self ($12.00)   _____

The Twelve Steps of Forgiveness ($10.00)   _____

The Circle of Atonement ($12.00)   _____

The Bridge to Reality ($12.00)   _____

From Ego to Self ($10.00)   _____

Virtues of the Way ($7.50)   _____

The Body of Truth ($7.50)   _____

Available Light ($10.00)   _____

Audio Tapes by Paul Ferrini

The Circle of Healing ($10.00)   _____

Healing the Wounded Child ($10.00)   _____

Forgiveness: The Original Blessing ($10.00)   _____

The Poetry of the Soul ($10.00)   _____

Seek First the Kingdom ($10.00)   _____

Answering Our Own Call for Love ($10.00)   _____

The Ecstatic Moment ($10.00)   _____

Honoring Self and Other ($10.00)   _____

Love Without Conditions ($19.95) 2 tapes   _____

Ending the Betrayal of the Self ($16.95) 2 tapes   _____

Relationships: Changing Past Patterns ($16.95) 2 tapes   _____

Relationship As a Spiritual Path ($16.95) 2 tapes   _____

Opening to Christ Consciousness ($16.95) 2 tapes   _____

Posters and Notecards

Risen Christ Poster 11"x17" ($10.00)   _____

Ecstatic Moment Poster 8.5"x11" ($5.00)   _____

Risen Christ Notecards 8/pkg ($10.00)   _____

Ecstatic Moment Notecards 8/pkg ($10.00)   _____

Shipping

($2.50 for first item, $1.00 each additional item.   _____

Add additional $1.00 for first class postage   _____

and an extra $1.00 for hardcover books.)   _____

MA residents please add 5% sales tax.   _____

Please allow 1-2 weeks for delivery   TOTAL   _____

Send Order To: Heartways Press P. O. Box 99,
Greenfield, MA 01302-0099   413-774-9474
Toll free: 1-888-HARTWAY (Orders only)